GERMAN BANKS
AND GERMAN ECONOMIC GROWTH
FROM UNIFICATION TO WORLD WAR I

This is a volume in the Arno Press collection

DISSERTATIONS IN EUROPEAN ECONOMIC HISTORY

See last pages of this volume for a complete list of titles.

GERMAN BANKS AND GERMAN ECONOMIC GROWTH FROM UNIFICATION TO WORLD WAR I

Hugh Neuburger

ARNO PRESS

A New York Times Company

New York / 1977

Editorial Supervision: ANDREA HICKS

First publication 1977 by Arno Press, Inc.

Reproduced from a copy in The University of Chicago Library

DISSERTATIONS IN EUROPEAN ECONOMIC HISTORY
ISBN for complete set: 0-405-10773-0
See last pages of this volume for titles.

Manufactured in the United States of America

Library of Congress Cataloging in Publication Data

Neuburger, Hugh M 1943-
German banks and German economic growth from unification to World War I.

(Dissertations in European economic history)
Originally presented as the author's thesis, University of Chicago, 1974.
Bibliography: p.
1. Banks and banking--Germany--History. 2. Germany--Economic conditions. I. Title. II. Series.
HG3048.N48 1977 332.1'0943 77-77182
ISBN 0-405-10795-1

THE UNIVERSITY OF CHICAGO

GERMAN BANKS AND GERMAN ECONOMIC GROWTH FROM UNIFICATION TO WORLD WAR I

A DISSERTATION SUBMITTED TO
THE FACULTY OF THE DIVISION OF THE SOCIAL SCIENCES
IN CANDIDACY FOR THE DEGREE OF
DOCTOR OF PHILOSOPHY

DEPARTMENT OF HISTORY

BY

HUGH NEUBURGER

CHICAGO, ILLINOIS

DECEMBER, 1974

ACKNOWLEDGEMENTS

The help of Professors Arcadius Kahan, William H. McNeill, Robert Fogel, Donald McCloskey, Leonard Krieger, Richard Zecher and Earl J. Hamilton is gratefully acknowledged. I also wish to thank Professor Houston H. Stokes with whom I collaborated in performing the econometric work that appears in Chapter IV.

TABLE OF CONTENTS

CHAPTER I

INTRODUCTION

Explanations of the character and remarkable speed of German industrialization commonly accent one feature of this process, the role of the German banking system. The "universal" or Kreditbanken comprise that part of the German banking system upon which such attention has focused. The complexity of the banker's art makes interpretations of the role of banking in German industrialization difficult to evaluate. In all three of their chief functions, intermediation, credit creation (through fractional reserve banking) and securities broking, banks make the savings of lenders available to borrowers. Having banks perform these functions gives rise to far lower transactions costs in a modern economy than having borrowers and lenders attempt to find each other without the banks' aid. Once a banking system is established however, the "quality" of its service to an economy and the bearing of that "quality" on economic development present formidable problems for which no generally accepted solutions exist.[1] Unlike the success of the banks in maximizing their own profits which could easily be determined with sufficient data, the success of the banks in serving the economy cannot be measured by any familiar technique. Particularly in the case of the question of the banks' effect on economic growth, which has always been

---

[1] In this context "quality" includes such factors as efficiency of credit allocation and provision of financial information and advice.

the liveliest issue in this regard, economic theory offers no guide. If there was such an effect, it was positive, negative or neutral, and much of the literature gives the impression that it was positive. More often than not discussions of this question have been written without benefit of statistical or econometric techniques, without archival evidence or without both. Yet in approaching such a question, both archival evidence about the relations of the banking system to industry and an econometric test of these relations can be used. Because archival evidence is of a different quality than econometric techniques, both approaches have their intrinsic advantages each may serve to supplement the findings of the other. It will also be useful to examine the roles of both private banks and corporate banks (*Kreditbanken*) and their places within the German banking system in order to understand the changes German banking experienced between 1879 and 1914.

Because of the unwillingness of the governments of the various German states to grant a corporate charter to a bank, there were before 1848 only private (i.e., non-incorporated) banking houses and state financial institutions in Germany.[1] In that year private banks were introduced to a new and potent competitor, the *Kreditbank*. The crisis of 1848 and the installation of the first constitutional government in Prussia allowed the Ministry of Trade to make a radical departure from earlier policy. In order to prevent the collapse of a major banking house in the Rhineland, A. Schaafhausen, and to alleviate the extreme

---

[1]For a discussion of the functions of private banks see Chapter II.

financial crisis in that region, the Ministry of Trade granted this bank a corporate charter. On August 28, the Schaafhausen banking firm of Cologne became the Schaafhausen'scher Bankverein. The granting of this charter was a revolutionary event in the development of German banking. The introduction of the joint-stock form allowed shares to be purchased by investors whose liability did not exceed the par value of the shares. Far greater sums could now be brought into play on a limited liability basis than those for which the partners in private banks would have wished to be personally liable.

Other bankers were not slow in seeking similar charters for themselves, but their enthusiasm was not universally shared. After the crisis of 1848 had passed and the conservative Prussian aristocracy and bureaucracy once more had firm control, the Prussian government was less willing to make concessions to middle-class interests and showed a stubborn disinclination to grant additional bank charters. The Discontogesellschaft, organized in Berlin in 1851, was given only very restricted bill discounting privileges and was not permitted to assume a semi-corporate form of organization (as a _Kommanditgesellschaft auf Aktien_) or to engage in the full range of banking functions until 1856.[1] The Berliner Handelsgesellschaft was granted a similar charter in the same year. Outside Prussia only one major institution was established in these years. The Pereires, founders of the Credit Mobilier, sought to form a similar institution in Germany in cooperation with friendly

---

[1]Under this corporate form the main partner (or partners) is fully liable but the liability of the silent partners is limited to the par value of the shares.

German interests. Blocked by local private bankers from obtaining a charter in Frankfurt, this group chose nearby Darmstadt where a charter was easily obtained. The Bank für Handel und Industrie, otherwise known as the Darmstädter Bank, began operations in 1853 with a very broad program directed particularly to railroad the other industrial promotion. It is clear that the Crédit Mobilier was the model for the Darmstädter Bank and perhaps for all Kreditbanken although this honor is sometimes given to the Schaafhausen'scher Bankverein.[1] In any case, the four German institutions referred to above remained the chief proponents of this new type of banking until 1870.

The formation of the North German Confederation and shortly thereafter of the Second Empire created new opportunities for German banking. With the introduction of a uniform commercial code during the 1870's and the establishment of the Reichsbank in 1876, conditions favored as never before the development of trade and finance on a national scale.[2] In response to these conditions and particularly to the boom conditions of the early 1870's, numerous banks were founded but only a few became major institutions. The charter of the Deutsche

---

[1]The Belgian Société Générale pour favoriser l' Industrie Nationale des Pays-Bas, founded in 1822, may well have been the model for both the German and French institutions. See R. Cameron, France and the Economic Development of Europe (Chicago: Rand, McNally, 1966) and J. Riesser, The Great German Banks and their Concentration (Washington: Government Printing Office, 1911).

[2]The establishment of the Reichsbank in 1876 was of central importance in this respect. The Reichsbank managed the currency and heavily influenced market interest rates with its discount rate. The Reichsbank did not hold bank reserves against deposits (which were not required); rather it stood ready to discount bills of exchange at all times thereby providing the banks with support in periods of stringency.

Bank was approved in March, 1870, and the bank opened its doors in Berlin the following month. Fostering foreign trade was the chief point of the program of the Deutsche Bank. In that same year the Commerz- und Disconto Bank began its operations in Hamburg. The Dresdner Bank started its career in 1872 building up a strong position in the region of Saxony and Thuringia. A last entry to the ranks of the major Kreditbanken was the Nationalbank für Deutschland which was founded in 1881. These eight banks comprised the core of joint-stock banking in Germany before World War I.

Kreditbanken are also referred to as Universalbanken or "universal banks." This term is an apt one because these banks combined functions that had never before been united in a single German financial institution. The functions of commercial banks, investment banks, development banks and investment trusts were all brought together in the Kreditbank. Until 1870 one aspect of commercial banking, deposit banking was practiced primarily by Sparkassen which were state or communally operated savings banks that extended credit to artisans and small businesses. Among the Kreditbanken the Deutsche Bank pioneered the policy of attracting deposits by opening special deposit offices in the early 1870's. During the 1880's and most clearly after 1890, the Kreditbanken achieved a complete fusion of commercial and investment banking. In German the phrase "regular business" denotes the full range of commercial banking functions. Appearing on a balance sheet under this heading as liabilities were demand deposits (payable without delay) and time deposits (payable only at specified intervals, the longest of which was six months). Appearing as assets were current-accounts, domestic and foreign bills discounted, acceptances and various categories of loans against securities and goods.[1] In the period from 1871 to 1913, bill discounting initially comprised the greater part of this business but by 1890 yielded the leading role to current-account credit. While such results were subject to considerable fluctuation, it appears that in this period roughly three-quarters of the total profits of the *Kreditbanken* were derived from commercial banking operations and the remaining quarter from brokerage commissions.[2]

From their earliest days, *Kreditbanken* were active in the field of investment banking, for which the German phrase is "irregular business." These banks acted as securities underwriters as well as brokers. In these roles the banks sold corporate and public securities of both domestic and foreign origin. Much of the trading on exchanges and of unlisted securities was executed by banks acting either on their own accounts or for others on commission. *Kreditbanken* issued and traded corporate bonds and shares, and securities, chiefly bonds of the imperial and state governments. Mortgage bonds (*Pfandbriefe*) were merely traded by *Kreditbanken* since they were issued by special mortgage banks.

---

[1]A current-account is a demand deposit account which may be overdrawn subject to terms and a credit limit agreed upon in opening the account; in such accounts interest is paid on credit balances and charged on debit balances. A bill of exchange is discounted when it is bought for its face value less interest to its due date. An acceptance is a draft on a bank by a firm (or individual) ordering the bank to pay a third party a specified amount at some future date (usually not more than six months following its issue). The drawer of the draft must pay the bank the amount of the draft plus interest when it comes due and usually provides some form of collateral until the due date.

[2]Riesser, p. 465.

Securities issue was organized on the basis of consortia, or syndicates, formed by groups of banks. That Kreditbank with the closest relations with a firm became the leader of the syndicate which floated the firm's securities. The leader in consultation with the firm the securities of which were being issued would choose the other banks to be included in the syndicate and offer each member bank a share of the total issue. The terms of sale were determined by the leader and agreed upon in contracts between the leader and each member. In very large issues, smaller banks could also take quotas "under" the group of major banks that comprised the syndicates for such larger issues.[1] Over the course of this era, Kreditbanken became the dominant forces in these syndicates.

Certain characteristics of the industrial financing of the Kreditbanken have been emphasized in descriptions of the activities of these banks by Gerschenkron and others.[2] Short-term credit had previously been intended for and had been primarily used for short-term purposes (i.e., for working capital rather than for fixed capital). In order to foster industrial development, Kreditbanken extended large amounts of short-term credit to industrial firms for long-term (fixed capital) purposes. Such lending was often accomplished through current-accounts under circumstances that allowed the distinction between long- and short-term credit to be blurred. The advantage of using current-accounts for long-term credit was that the banks continued to adhere in a technical

---

[1] In such cases the smaller banks bore none of the responsibility of making the issues. Under the law only banks signing a prospectus for an issue bore responsibility and these smaller banks did not ordinarily sign.

[2] Alexander Gerschenkron, Economic Backwardness in Historical Perspective (Cambridge: Harvard University Press, 1962), p. 14.

sense to the rule that banks should extend short-term credit only. Of course, a short-term loan that was regularly renewed may have been quite as desirable as a long-term loan to a capital hungry firm. Firms just beginning operations or needing capital in depression periods when securities were very difficult to sell may have had very little chance of raising capital by securities issue. In such situations current-account credit offered by Kreditbanken was surely an attractive way of obtaining capital. Although attractive to many firms, this use of current-account credit posed obvious risks to the banks. Large sums were committed to firms which provided little if any liquid backing for these loans. Usually only such illiquid assets as land, plant and equipment were pledged as collateral for these loans. What compensated the banks for bearing such risks were the handsome returns earned by transforming current-account debt into securities and selling them. This process began as soon as the market had enough confidence in the borrowing firms to accept their securities.

Risk-taking of this kind required that a bank maintain close contact with the borrowing firm. For this reason, banks that were major creditors of a firm or that held large quotas in the syndicates that issued a firm's securities received seats on the firm's board of directors (Aufsichtsrat). Often the bank representatives on these boards held both the position of chairman and that of vice-chairman, further enhancing their influence among their colleagues. In 1905 Riesser counted 819 representatives of the eight previously mentioned banks on the boards of directors of German industrial firms.[1] Hence, from both the standpoint of personnel

---

[1] Riesser, pp. 897-920.

and of range of services performed, _Kreditbanken_ enjoyed very intimate relations with the firms they served.

Close relations with industries that were beginning to operate on a national scale soon required of banks the capacity to serve industry on this scale. For the four major _Kreditbanken_ originally based outside of Berlin, the establishment of that city as the premier center in Germany of political and economic power in 1871 made the opening of offices there imperative. These banks were also drawn to Berlin by the predominance of the Berlin bourse which gradually forced the Frankfurt bourse and the other German exchanges into the role of mere provincial financial centers.[1] Yet there were centrifugal as well as centripetal forces acting on these banks. Throughout the period, the banks established provincial branches in an effort to achieve the broadest possible geographical dispersion. Only the Berliner Handelsgesellschaft abstained from branch banking, clinging instead to unitary banking. Under the unitary system, administrative control was tighter and malfeasance easier to prevent than under the branch banking system. Once deposit banking had been accepted by the _Kreditbanken_, however, banks with branches were far better able to gather deposits and to help industries located or wishing to locate far from financial centers.

Private banks competed vigorously with the _Kreditbanken_, especially at the regional or local level. The _Kreditbanken_ dealt with this competition by absorbing private banks in large numbers. When

---

[1] G. von Schulze-Gaevernitz, _Die deutsche Kreditbank_, V, No. II of _Grundriss der Sozialökonomik_ (Tubingen: Mohr, 1922), 35.

outright absorption was not employed, the *Kreditbanken* arranged *commandites* (partnerships) or community of interest agreements to cement good relations with private banks. If a connection proved viable, absorption usually followed. By 1913 all of the major *Kreditbanken* which chose branch banking had extensive networks of branches with varying geographical emphases. The business of these branches came substantially at the expense of the private banks. Economies of scale may explain much of the success of the *Kreditbanken* in this competition with private banks. In any case, geographical expansion made the major *Kreditbanken* forces of national scope.

What held at the national level held equally well for the international. For those engaged in foreign trade the services of a *Kreditbank* were invaluable. In some cases banks actually established branches abroad, as did the Deutsche Bank in London. Foreign representation was also arranged by founding separate institutions, like the Deutsch-Überseeische Bank, a subsidiary of the Deutsche Bank whose purpose was to facilitate German trade with South America. At the very least, *Kreditbanken* had good working relations with major banks in foreign business centers and remained *au courant* concerning foreign economic conditions. Foreign contacts were scarcely novel in banking, but their depth and scale in Germany after 1870 came to extend far beyond previous experience.

All of these factors must be seen against the background of that factor which made the other meaningful: capital strength. A quick glance at the share capital of the eight major *Kreditbanken* reveals why they were a force to be reckoned with. In 1908 this capital amounted to

1,024 million marks (about 50 million pounds) indicating an enormous lending potential.[1] The opportunity that limited liability charters gave to Kreditbanken to amass huge amounts of capital was exploited by them with great success. Such success meant that by 1914 the private banks existed in the shadow of their powerful new competitors.

This transition within German banking from 1848 to 1914 had consequences of the greatest magnitude. Since the period of this transition was substantially the same as that of the industrialization of Germany, some serious questions arise about the interrelationship of these two phenomena. As the charters of Kreditbanken like the Schaafhausen'scher Bankverein show, a prime motive for the founding of Kreditbanken was to make industrial loans, loans that most private banks found too risky to make. Primarily because of lack of alternative sources of capital, industry chose to borrow massively from the Kreditbanken, and these banks chose to make the loans.[2] The pattern which these facts suggest is one of symbiotic growth.[3] Characterizing the development of this symbiosis from the banks' side is a demanding task. To describe the transition within German banking, one must first have a point of departure.

---

[1]Since these banks had no reserve requirement against deposits, it is not possible to estimate this lending potential exactly. It should merely be noted that on December 31, 1908, cash on hand in all Kreditbanken amounted to 8 per cent of credits on current-account and deposits (not including acceptances). To make a comparison with Britain, note that after 1875 the Bank of England could issue notes up to 15 million pounds backed by first class securities; all note issues beyond this limit had to be backed by equal amounts of gold bullion. The capital of the eight major Kreditbanken was over three times greater than this limit.

[2]In extending current-account credit to industry, these banks granted short-term credit at short-term rates but renewed the credit in a manner that made it virtually indistinguishable from long-term credit.

[3]Werner Sombart, Das Wirtschaftsleben im Zeitalter des Hochkapitalismus (Munich: Duncker und Humblot, 1928), p. 754.

This point may be sought in the private bank. What was its role? How did it relate to industry and to the _Kreditbanken_? How great was its capacity for adaptation? The archives of Gebrüder Bethmann in Frankfurt can shed some light on these questions. After a point of departure has been fixed, it becomes possible to explore the path that was taken. That path, of course, is that of the _Kreditbanken._ What was the character of their relations with industry and with other banks? How did their operations change? The archives of the Deutsche Bank offer indications as to how such questions can be answered.

The use of archival materials to account for the transition within German banking and the relevance of this transition to industry presents difficulties as well as opportunities. Closeness to these institutions and richness of detail about them can provide a sharply focused picture of each type of bank; however, this picture cannot be safely generalized for all banks of that type. Can a more general picture be obtained? In the case of the private banks, only an archival approach may be pursued because data series relating to them are not available. The absence of these data series poses no grave problem for examining the place of these banks in industrial development since, with certain exceptions, private banks did not play a prominent role in that process. In investigating the role of the _Kreditbanken_, an alternative approach has recently become possible. By collecting a reliable data series on the _Kreditbanken_ for the years 1883 to 1913, Ekkehard Eistert provided the essential material needed for such an approach. In _Die Beeinflussung des Wirtschaftswachstums in Deutschland von 1883 bis 1913 durch das Bankensystem_, he treats this question using economic theory and statistical analysis.[1] One of his more important conclusions is that the credit policy of these banks was either a necessary condition for or a facilitating factor in the growth of Germany industry.[2] Interesting as this approach and its results are, some fundamental issues are left unexplored.

Econometric methods offer a means by which one such issue may be examined. Since it is the task of banks to allocate credit, one way of interpreting the claim that the Kreditbanken furthered German economic growth is to say that they allocated credit efficiently. The question of the banks' influence on growth becomes measurable when put in these terms. An econometric model has been constructed using a production function to measure the efficiency of allocation of bank credit to the German non-agricultural economy from 1883 to 1913. The model indicates that the Kreditbanken were allocating credit (i.e., current-account credit) in a manner that inhibited rather than stimulated the growth of non-agricultural output and prevented non-agricultural output from reaching a level that would have been reached with a more competitive capital market. On the basis of this model, a macro-economic interpretation of German banking can be developed which applies to all Kreditbanken. This interpretation can be supplemented by analyzing the non-pecuniary services of the banks to industry (including provision of information and management consulting) and by analyzing the effect of these services. Should these services appear significant, they may be used together with results of the econometric model to fashion a broader interpretation of the place

---

[1]Berlin: Duncker und Humblot, 1970.

[2]Ibid., p. 170.

Kreditbanken held in German economic growth. Such a combination of archival and econometric methods makes it possible not only to present a useful account of the changes that occurred within German banking before World War I, but also to assess the meaning of those changes.

CHAPTER II

THE PRIVATE BANK:
GEBRÜDER BETHMANN OF FRANKFURT

If public or semi-public institutions are excluded, the term "bank" has had a reasonably clear meaning in Germany from the early modern period until approximately 1850. The banks of that age were firms whose _principal_ activity was to invest their own funds and funds deposited with them at interest and payable on short notice in short-term loans against a safe and liquid type of security. Such banks were referred to as _Privatbanken_ or private banks and their chief task was commercial banking. The main instrument they relied upon was the bill of exchange, well-suited to their need for safety, liquidity and a short length of run. Normally, loans with a longer length of run were considered unsafe and were avoided with exception of state debt which banks issued, sold to investors and held on their own account. As their English name indicates, these banks existed mainly to provide credit to local, regional and, in major trade centers, international commerce. The aid that private banks gave to commerce was a significant contribution to German economic development because commerce was important both in its own right and as a helpful precondition for industrialization.

Issuing and dealing in state debt was a more narrowly financial function of private banks. During the eighteenth century, state loans in Germany were increasingly in the form of negotiable securities the issue of which was arranged by "court factors" (Hoffaktoren), often Jews.[1] Issue of securities was followed by trading of securities in organized markets of which that of Amsterdam provided a model in the eighteenth century and that of Frankfurt a good example in the nineteenth. The brokers in these markets were private bankers. Among the best known in Frankfurt were the Rothschilds and the Bethmanns whose rise to prominence was in large measure a result of their involvement in state finance. The familiar story of the Rothschilds' skillful manoevering while serving the various participants in the Napoleonic wars need not be repeated here. It need merely be noted that the success of private bankers as securities brokers and supply contractors greatly enhanced their positions and that of Frankfurt as a financial center.

As a free imperial city, Frankfurt had a long, tradition as a commerical center. By the early nineteenth century, it had become the chief German money and securities market. As early as 1800, 20 different state securities were regularly traded on its exchange.[2] The pivotal role of the Rothschilds in much of the securities issue of Central Europe, in particular, of Austria, lent further importance to Frankfurt and intensified its ties to the other major European financial centers during the years 1820 to 1848. Yet the focus of Frankfurt's economy remained commerce of a quite traditional kind and this tendency

---

[1] For a good discussion of the role of Jewish private bankers in the commercial life of Frankfurt see: H. Kirchholtes, Jüdische Privatbanken in Frankfurt am Main (Frankfurt: Verlag von Waldemar Kramer, 1969).

[2] Schulze-Gaevernitz, p. 29.

was especially evident in banking. What innovation there was in Germany before 1850 to hasten industrialization and facilitate industrial financing occurred primarily in the Rhineland. Tilly has described the progressive role played by banks like Oppenheim and von der Heydt, Kersten in early Rhenish industrialization.[1] In Frankfurt the atmosphere was decidedly different. A pronounced antipathy to industry of the modern type and to the joint-stock form prevailed through much of the nineteenth century.

The source of this antipathy was a firm attachment to the traditional commerce from which so many private banks stemmed. The markets for long-traded commodities like textiles and wine were familiar unlike those for new manufactured goods. Furthermore, a private bank operated within the framework of an ethic to which the notion of limited liability was anathema and in which a good name was essential. Carl Fürstenberg, for many years the leading figure of the Berliner Handelsgesellschaft, recalled the prevalent outlook with a quotation from his employer in the days of his commercial apprenticeship (the 1860's): "Angefragtes Haus ist ein Sch . . . haus."[2] In other words, a very dim view was taken of not paying one's obligations and of legal devices like limited liability which carried too strong a connotation of possible default. And, of course, the great strength of such banks as Rothschild and Bethmann was that their reputations were beyond reproach. These banks had an additional

---

[1] Richard Tilly, Financial Institutions and Industrialization in the Rhineland, 1815-1870 (Madison: University of Wisconsin Press, 1966).

[2] Carl Fürstenberg, Die Lebensgeschichte eines deutschen Bankiers (Wiesbaden: Rheinische Verlags-Anstalt, 1961), p. 12.

ground for reluctance to finance modern industry. To the extent that new factory industry was capital intensive, which it generally was in Germany, the profitable financing of public debt seemed to be threatened since it was feared that the capital market would not bear both state and industrial finance on a large scale.[1] State securities were considered much safer than corporate securities. Given the greater attractiveness of government and commercial finance, the private banks of Frankfurt did not devote much effort to financing modern industrial development.

In the Frankfurt banking community, Gebrüder Bethmann had a prominent place. While not so venerable as a firm like Koch, Lauteren and Co. which dated from 1586, Bethmann was respectably old having been established in 1748 as an outgrowth of the trading firm of Jacob Adami, which itself went back to 1700. Although less stunning than that of the Rothschilds, the rise of the Bethmanns was rapid by conventional standards. The origins of this rise can be traced to the career of Johann Philipp Bethmann (1715-1793), court banker to Maria Theresa. Under his leadership Gebrüder Bethmann became a mainstay of the Austrian treasury; the bank floated Autrian loans that totaled in the tens of millions of florins by the end of the Napoleonic wars. Bethmann's rise continued during the career of Simon Moritz von Bethmann (1768-1826) whose prominence is shown by his designation as the representative of the city of Frankfurt to the Congress of Vienna. In the period before 1820, he arranged loans

---

[1] On the question of supply of capital, Borchardt takes the view that capital scarcity was not a problem. See: Knut Borchardt, "Zur Frage des Kapitalmangels in der ersten Hälfte des 19. Jahrhunderts in Deutschland," Jahrbücher für Nationalökonomie und Statistik, CLXXIII (1961): 401-421.

to Russia, Denmark, Sweden, the Kingdom of Westphalia and various small German states. Such state loans along with commercial lending and trading in commodities accounted for most of Bethmann's activities in the Napoleonic and Restoration eras.

Financing modern industry was certainly not a field of investment in which Bethmann showed much interest.[1] Industrial finance was much too risky for Gebrüder Bethmann, which was among the more conservative banks of a quite conservative financial community. One possible exception was Bethmann's participation in 1826 in the financing of the Rhine-Main Steamship Company. But this venture did not prove viable and had to be dissolved in 1832. Railroads constituted a major exception to Bethmann's practice of avoiding industrial financing but a serious problem of interpretation arises here. Considering the frequency with which railroad securities bore some kind of state guaranty, they cannot as a group be considered purely private corporate obligations. How much did a railroad bond with a state guaranty differ from the state loans with which Bethmann had so much experience? Such securities were clearly similar. Given this aspect of railroad financing, Bethmann's reluctance to participate in industrial finance does not appear to have conflicted with extensive participation in railroad development. Prior to 1870 other examples of industrial financing by Bethmann are few and far between. As did other prominent private banks, Bethmann played a part in the establishment and conduct of affairs (as a director) of banks like the Frankfurter Bank, the Bank für Handel und Industrie, and the Bank für Suddeutschland.

---

[1]Udo E. G. Heyn, "Private Banking and Industrialization: The Case of Frankfurt am Main, 1825-1875" (unpublished Ph.D. dissertation, Department of Economics, University of Wisconsin, 1969).

Through such participations Bethmann had, at best, an indirect part in industrial finance.

The attitude of the Frankfurt commercial community toward industrial finance is a matter of some significance. It bears repeating that until the 1870's the foremost securities and money market in Germany was at Frankfurt. Moreover, throughout the nineteenth century that city remained the seat of many of Germany's leading private banks. The strength of Frankfurt as a financial center represented a potential for fostering industrial growth far exceeding that of the Rhenish banks in spite of the progresssive outlook and financing practices that characterized the Rhineland. It has already been shown that in the case of Gebrüder Bethmann before 1870 this potential went substantially unrealized. In order to understand better Bethmann's role in post-1870 German economic development and that of the many private banks cast in a similar mold, it is necessary to examine Bethmann's relations with industry in the post-1870 era. Since Bethmann dealt extensively with the *Kreditbanken* in matters relating to industry, these inter-bank relations must also be explored. What is to be sought in this inquiry is some notion of the extent of change in Bethmann's operations and that among like institutions. On this basis a judgment can be made about both the potential and the actual contribution of Bethmann and its like to economic growth in an era of continuing industrialization.

Among the post-1870 files of the Bethmann Archive which relate to industry, material relating to securities issue predominates heavily so that an effort to deal with the questions raised above must be based on this material.[1] A striking fact of which familiarity with the archive soon makes one aware is that Bethmann rarely had a leading role in the promotion of industrial securities in the period 1870 to 1913. The bank was often a member of syndicates led by the major Berlin banks and on occasion "sub-participant" (Unterbeteiligte) taking a position in a securities issue from a local bank that was a full member of the syndicate. The reasons for Bethmann's failure to play a major role in industrial company promotion are evident. Unfamiliarity with industry, particularly with industrial technology, and lingering distaste for and perhaps also distrust of the joint-stock form surely loomed large. The mood that followed the crash of 1873, with its numerous revelations of swindles, intensified the Bethmanns' innate conservatism in this regard. A second reason was Bethmann's size. Because private banks did not make public annual statements of condition, the extent to which capital strength was a constraint is not fully clear but it is clear that Bethmann and the major Berlin Kreditbanken were orders of magnitude apart in this respect. As the Frankfurt exchange lost its leading position to Berlin, that too made industrial company promotion less attractive in Frankfurt. These factors notwithstanding, Bethmann did in several instances take a major part in company promotions and it is these instances that will first be examined.

In the spring of 1881, Bethmann became interested in the Hallberger publishing firm of Stuttgart. Its owner had recently died and his heirs decided to convert the firm into a joint-stock company. The

---

[1] The Bethmann Archive is in the custody of the Frankfurt Stadtarchiv and is open to the public.

project was brought to Raphael Erlanger and Sons, a prosperous Frankfurt private bank, by a broker who specialized in finding financial support for such conversions. In turn Erlanger took the matter to Bethmann who was favorably impressed, especially with recent annual profits of the firm. A letter of Moritz von Bethmann, the leading figure of Gebrüder Bethmann in this period, to his nephew, Hugo von Bethmann (in Paris) of May 10, 1881, provides some insight into the elder Bethmann's view of the matter.[1] In order to be sure of the character and reputation of the publishing firm, he checked with Jügel, a well-known Frankfurt publisher, whose reply was quite favorable. Considerable importance was attached to the fact that the Hallberger family was to retain a large holding in the firm and to continue in its management. The tone of the letter conveys the elder Bethmann's confidence in the solidity of the venture but not without suggesting that concern for the propriety of a stock issue of this sort was also a consideration.

What sort of concern was indicated? Apparently Bethmann was worried about the good name of any banker engaged in company promotion. "Don't be afraid of a stock issue!," he advises his nephew.[2] Later he reassures his nephew that "this is not the sort of stock issue that one has to be ashamed of."[3] If Bethmann took so cautious a view of the conversion of a successful publishing firm, what must he have thought of high-risk projects involving new, untested technology? It is unlikely

---

[1] Bethmann Archiv, V, 753.

[2] "Erschrecke nicht uber die Gründung!"

[3] "Man brauchte sich also mit einer solchen Gründung nicht zu schamen."

that such projects would have been considered appropriate for Gebrüder Bethmann. Even the tone of correspondence within the Bethmann family points up the extraordinary conservatism of banking policy, especially in matters like securities issue.

The correspondence from uncle to nephew continued with a letter of May 12, 1881, in which the project was reviewed in greater detail and Hugo von Bethmann was offered a seat on the board of directors (Aufsichtsrat) of the new corporation. Mortiz von Bethmann again noted the good impression which the venture had made on him and on Ludwig Erlanger, who had already accepted a seat on the firm's board. The younger Bethmann was also reminded that the Hallberger family would continue its connection with the firm "so that the world won't be able to construe the thing as pure stock-jobbing (Agiotage)." Far from urging his nephew to accept the seat for the good of the Bethmann house, the elder Bethmann advised that the decision be made solely on the basis of convenience "since from the business point of view the house sees no value in the entry of one of its associates in an industrial establishment. . . ."[1] It was not as if the position were dishonorable; in that case it would never have been offered. Rather it was not a matter about which a distinguished private banking family need show much concern.

Hugo von Bethmann accepted his uncle's offer and his reasons for accepting were given in a letter of May 13, 1881, to Moritz von Bethmann. Although he had reservations, the advantages outweighed them. In a carefully balanced assessment he comments:

---

[1]". . . das Haus, von geschäftlichen Standpunkt aus, keinen Werth auf den Eintritt eines Associes in ein industrielles Etablement legt . . ."

> Even if today when all the consequences cannot be appraised, I do not feel any special inclination to enter new firms [as a member of the supervisory board] particularly when they are located elsewhere, I cannot conceal the fact that there are now great advantages in widening one's business circle. And directorships often bring connections and relations which can be valuable, while through complete abstinence one can easily isolate oneself more and more which under conditions like those in Frankfurt appears very disadvantageous. Uncle Franz [Borgnis] surely never wanted directorships for himself other than that of the [Bethmann] house which certainly kept him sufficiently occupied; yet he was not against it in principle if someone in the house showed a special desire. Since you are clearly not seeking this kind of activity, I will for my part gladly accept this role. . . .

In contrasting his own views with those of another uncle, also a partner in Gebrüder Bethmann, Hugo von Bethmann illustrated the slow transition occurring within the private banks. Rather than find himself isolated and unable to take part in business opportunities, he was prepared to adapt to the new business environment of joint-stock companies and industrial ventures. Yet he was acutely conscious of being eased by the older generation into a transition that its members had not the inclination to make themselves.

In the most important respects, the Bethmanns made a wise choice in financing the Hallberger conversion. The syndicate for the sale of 1,500,000 marks of stock of the Deutsche Verlagsanstalt, the new name of the firm, was a success. Prestigious private banks like Jacob S. H. Stern and D. and J. de Neufville as well as prominent individuals like A. Niederhofheim, a director of the Darmstädter Bank, took substantial participations in the syndicate. The records of the syndicate reveal that it was quite successful showing a net profit of about 12.5 per cent on the shares that were distributed (in this case, 45 per cent of the total shares). An option was exercized increasing the number of shares available to the leading banks and still higher profits were realized on shares withheld for later sale. Furthermore, the dividends of the Deutsche Verlagsanstalt averaged 12 per cent in the five years after incorporation, a result with which all involved must have been very pleased.

In only one respect did this conversion prove disappointing to Gebrüder Bethmann. The letters of Hugo von Bethmann to his uncle show that he became quite accustomed to his new role as a member of the board of the Deutsche Verlagsanstalt and his term ran until 1886. When in 1885 he was unceremoniously forced out of the supervisory board, the Bethmanns must have been quite unpleasantly surprised. It seems that the Hallbergers wanted to use the seat to cement relations with someone they felt was more useful to the firm. In his letter of March 4, 1885, explaining the situation to his nephew, Mortiz von Bethmann wrote that he did not want to prejudge the matter but ". . . I know what I would do." The elder Bethmann advised a quiet withdrawal. For bankers of the traditional type getting accustomed to the newer methods and outlook of corporate capitalism was not always an easy affair.

The Bethmanns were soon to learn firsthand that industrial finance was not without serious risk. In the winter of 1888-1889 Gebrüder Bethmann again became involved as one of the leading banks in the conversion of an industrial firm to a joint-stock company. The firm, which was located in the small Rhineland town of Sürth near Cologne, was the

H. Hammerschmidt Machine Factory whose products were chiefly compressors, pumps, vessels and other equipment used in brewing. A relatively full record makes it possible to trace the course of the conversion in detail and to observe Bethmann's subsequent relations with the other banks involved and with the company. The project was recommended to Bethmann by Hermann Kahn of the firm of Kahn and Co. of Frankfurt. In the first correspondence concerning the conversion, a letter of January 28, 1889, from Bethmann to Kahn, the former agrees provisionally to participate in the project with a quota of ten per cent of the shares or "in the event that S. Oppenheim Jr. and Co. or the Schaafhausen'scher Bankverein or another house of equal standing should agree to act as an issuing bank, we accept with a share equal to that which the other house reserves for itself."[1] Bethmann's attitude was doubtless influenced by its unfamiliarity with industry and its hope that a bank more experienced in the field would evaluate the conversion and stand behind it.

When the Oppenheims committed themselves to the project, that supplied the sort of name and expertise that the Bethmanns thought was needed. An effort was made to bring B. H. Goldschmidt, a well-regarded Frankfurt banking firm, in to the affair, but it refused. Adolf Goldschmidt's refusal provides a most revealing echo of Bethmann's earlier ambivalence about the Deutsche Verlagsanstalt conversion. In an almost apologetic tone, Goldschmidt explained his firm's longstanding policy not to act as an issuing bank for industrial securities and surveyed the favorable outlook for the project indicated by the prevalent bull market,

---

[1] Bethmann Archiv, V, 568-569.

abundance of credit and political stability ("with the disappearance of Boulanger").[1] "In spite of all we cannot convince ourselves to make an industrial security issue, even with your very esteemed house." He concluded by accepting a subordinate participation of one hundred thousand marks. In 1889 an industrial firm in Germany was scarcely the novelty that it had been a half century earlier, yet the private banks of Frankfurt were still reacting to industrial securities issues as if they bore some secret taint; hence, Goldschmidt's rejection and Bethmann's somewhat hesitant acceptance.

The critical point upon which the attitude of the private banker may be summed up in one phrase, "moral responsibility." In contrast to taking a subordinate participation in an issuing syndicate in which a bank's role was to a great extent merely that of an agent of the issuing banks, issuing a security (i.e., being an Emittent or issuing bank) carried with it legal and also a broader moral responsibility. At the very outset of the conversion when Bethmann telegraphed acceptance to Oppenheim (in Cologne), it was done on condition that the latter accept the "moral responsibility."[2] Why did Gebrüder Bethmann show such reluctance to accept this responsibility? The answer may be sought in a subsequent letter of Bethmann to Oppenheim:

> We believe that we should not conceal from you that we surmounted earlier doubts arising from our complete unfamiliarity with the field of industry involved, the small sum for an official issue and all it entails, the

---

[1] Letter from Adolf Goldschmidt, partner in the banking firm of B. H. Goldschmidt, Frankfurt am Main, April 3, 1889 (Bethmann Archiv, V, 568-569).

[2] Telegram of March 30, 1889 (Bethmann Archiv, V, 568-569).

> abundant founding of firms recently and so forth only because we can follow you with complete confidence and because of the satisfaction of issuing in common with your honored house.[1]

In other words, Bethmann wanted Oppenheim to take the lead and the responsibility because of the former's inability to assess fully this kind of industrial project.

Bethmann's conduct in the affair substantiates this view. According to the correspondence between Bethmann and Oppenheim, the appraisal of the Sürth firm and the analysis of its operations was left entirely to Oppenheim and Kahn, chiefly to the former. The technical report on the firm is not in the file and all indicates suggest that Bethmann neither requested nor received it. There is a copy of the statutes proposed for the firm which were examined and approved by the Bethmanns' attorney. There is also a <u>Gutachten</u> (expert opinion) from an auditor, one Herr Lahnstein, which analyzes Hammerschmidt's books from 1885 to 1888. In the auditor's report the value of the inventory is estimated and there are comments on the quality and paying habits of customers and the arrangements with the firm's sales agents. Rather cursory profit statements for these years are included and show that the firm was earning 26 to 27 per cent per year after deductions for depreciation. Here was information that Bethmann could properly evaluate and the impression it made must have been a very positive one. Whether or not it sufficed is another question, for the success of an industrial firm depends on more than commercial considerations.

Bethmann simply left the matter of evaluating the technical

---

[1]Copy of a letter signed only "Gebrüder Bethmann," Frankfurt am Main, April 1, 1889 (<u>Bethmann Archiv</u>, V, 568-569).

expert's report to the Oppenheims. When Bethmann was informed in mid-April, 1889, that "the report of the technical expert satisfies the Oppenheims completely," he was equally satisfied.[1] It is not surprising that Gebrüder Bethmann was willing to trust a banking house like Sal. Oppenheim Jr. and Co. with its half century of experience in industrial finance, especially when the Oppenheims were taking a 40 per cent share of the conversion. Certainly the 400,000 to 500,000 marks that the Oppenheims were risking could be taken as a sign of confidence in the venture.[2] The Oppenheims' confidence notwithstanding, there is no denying that the Bethmanns could not get a direct, independent assessment within their own house of all aspects of the Hammerschmidt firm's operations, nor would this be possible in the future since they chose not to be represented on the new corporation's supervisory board. Whatever the Bethmanns lacked in knowledge necessarily increased the risk to them of making the conversion.

Initially the conversion went well and there appeared to be no cause for concern. The formalities were completed by mid-May. The subscription for the shares which took place on May 22 and May 23 was over-subscribed by a large margin reflecting the interest of both serious investors and speculators in the shares. It was usual in such cases for large blocks to be subscribed by speculators in the hope of making quick gains in the period following issue of the shares when the issuing banks

---

[1]Letter of Hermann Kahn of the banking firm of Kahn and Co. of Frankfurt am Main, Cologne, April 17, 1889 (Bethmann Archiv, V., 568-569).

[2]The share of Bethmann and Oppenheim was 40 per cent each or 412,000 marks but each also held an option on 80,000 marks in additional shares (at par). Kahn took the remaining 20 per cent.

"managed" the share price. Since the shares were admitted to both the Frankfurt and the Cologne exchanges, both Bethmann and Oppenheim had some "managing" to do. After eliminating from the list of subscribers those thought to be speculators, Bethmann and Kahn were able to distribute (zuteilen) all of the shares reserved for Frankfurt and Oppenheim had about fifty shares left in Cologne. Then the shares faced the test of the market supported, if need be, by the issuing banks.

This test did not prove an easy one. The shares were offered by the issuing syndicate to subscribers at 140 per cent (of par) and the support price, initially set at 145 per cent, was soon reduced to 140 per cent.[1] In the months following issue the market apparently did not find the shares of the Sürther Maschinenfabrik very attractive because the issuing syndicate had to buy large numbers of shares to maintain the support price. Then in mid-October, 1889, Bethmann got the first of a series of unpleasant surprises. The firm's projected dividend for the year was reduced from 14 or 15 per cent to 10 per cent, a return on investor's capital which in Bethmann's view did not justify a price of 140. Since considerable resources were used by the syndicate to keep the share price at that level, Bethmann was quite irritated. This irritation was not lessened by the fact that Kahn had been pleading for a lower support price since July and had been refused because of Oppenheim's assurances that the price was appropriate. Oppenheim replied with a long discourse on the high premiums other industrial shares were enjoying and accompanied it with suitable examples. Although he claimed that the

[1] The par value of the shares was 1,000 marks.

Sürther shares should rightly have been selling at a still higher premium, Oppenheim acceded to his colleagues' request that the price be allowed to fall somewhat. The market's buffeting of these shares was certainly more informative to Bethmann than Oppenheim's discourse.

Yet it would be misleading to paint the situation in too dark colors. When the syndicate agreement expired in December, 1889, its profit was computed and distributed. It amounted to about 34 per cent on the nominal capital of the issue. Bethmann's record lists a net profit of almost 32 per cent, although substantial sales to Bethmann partners are included which make this figure less meaningful than it otherwise would have been. Such profits are clearly satisfactory and the parties to the syndicate found them so. They agreed to continue the syndicate for another six months, to carry the unsold shares on the books at 125 per cent (instead of 140 per cent) and to lower the support price to 130. The syndicate had given some ground but was still very much a going affair.

During the next two years the syndicate operated uneventfully and was renewed in a perfunctory way. Because 1890 was a good year for the Sürther Maschinenfabrik, the syndicate was able to sell a substantial part of its remaining shares at favorable prices. The 11 per cent dividend for 1890 presumably satisfied the shareholders. During 1891 the syndicate was almost dormant. It entered the market very rarely to set the price of the shares and then only by prior agreement among the members. By the end of 1891, the syndicate had had two and a half years of reasonably satisfactory operations although it was left with a block of almost 100 unsold or repurchased Sürther shares. At this juncture,

Gebrüder Bethmann had no reason to regret its involvement in the conversion; soon it would have many.

Early in 1892 Bethmann was informed that the audit of the Sürther accounts for the previous year showed a loss and that without the intervention of the issuing banks no dividend would be paid. The difficulties of the firm were apparently caused by Hammerschmidt's mismanagement. The relevation of the firm's troubles was accompanied by very serious ill feeling between Kahn and Oppenheim with each attributing the responsibility for the problem to the other. On a superficial level the dispute centered on the presumed deficiences of the firm in 1889 and on the faulty decision made because of them. Each traced the negligence to the door of the other.[1] The central question was who would pay and how much in order that the firm could remain in business and pay a dividend. Kahn went so far as to consult an attorney and the notes of the meeting suggest that he was even prepared to accuse Oppenhem of being an accessory to a fraud (Beihülfe zum Betrug). To the Oppenheims such charges had a most unpleasant ring but they produced the result desired by the Oppenheims' colleagues who felt that the Oppenheims had a special responsibility in the affair. The Oppenheims acknowledged that responsibility.

Arrangements were worked out between Kahn and Oppenheim to which Bethmann readily gave his assent. The three issuing banks of the original syndicate formed a special syndicate to purchase a patent from the Sürther Maschinenfabrik. Knowledge of the purchase was closely guarded and the company continued to act as its owner. Kahn paid 6,000 marks, Bethmann

---

[1] Kahn alleged that a prior confidential relationship existed between Hammerschmidt and Oppenheim.

10,000 marks and Oppenheim 64,000 marks, so that 80,000 marks was paid for a patent which, according to Kahn, no longer had any market value. This arrangment allowed the company to pay a 5 per cent dividend for 1891. As a stop-gap measure, the patent purchase succeeded. There followed a change of management and, of course, a sharp drop in the price of the shares. Events were gradually making the costs of relatively uniformed investments in industry clearer to Bethmann.

In the hope of seeing the company return to profitable operation, the syndicate continued to function. As a part of the arrangements detailed above, Oppenheim committed himself to continuing its part in the syndicate's "management" of the Sürther share price. The support price originally mentioned was 85, but no action was taken until 1893. In that year the Sürther Maschinenfabrik paid no dividend at all. During the course of 1893, the syndicate did support the price of the shares with small purchases eventually allowing it to fall below 50. These purchases continued in 1894 despite the absence of any improvement of the firm's fortunes and a second omission of a dividend. A report of Kahn to the firm in April, 1894, gives some indication of why the syndicate's hopes for improvement were frustrated. In the period during which Hammerschmidt was running the firm, he is reported to have signed contracts with highly disadvantageous terms to which losses of 200,000 marks were attributed. As a consequence of these difficulties, the firm was contracting an increasingly large debt to Oppenheim. The situation called for some sort of action by the supervisory board and a number of plans to remedy the situation were proposed.

German commercial law provided several ways to accomplish the reorganization (<u>Sanierung</u>) of a company. Oppenheim favored issuing new shares to raise additional capital.[1] Bethmann thought that liquidation bonds or <u>Genusscheine</u> were preferable.[2] A third method involved the reduction of the value of the shares by a fixed percentage after which the shares could only be brought back to nominal value by a special payment equal to the percentage by which the shares' value was reduced. None of these possibilities was settled on during 1894 and another year passed without a dividend having been paid. Finally in March, 1895, S. Alfred Oppenheim proposed a solution based on the third of the methods mentioned above. By supplying the firm with additional capital, he sought to rid it of the debt it was carrying from previous operating losses and to enable it to pay a dividend for a least one year. The object of the plan was to allow the syndicate to "unload" (<u>abstiessen</u>) its remaining shares. To make the proposal more attractive to Bethmann, Oppenheim offered to join the Sürther supervisory board and, by implication, take a more direct role in the firm's affairs if his plan was accepted. The entry of technical expert, presumably an engineer, named J. L. Langeloth was also tied to the acceptance of the plan.

On the recommendation of Oppenheim and the technical expert he had brought in, Bethmann agreed to the reorganization plan. It was a costly step since under the plan's terms each shareholder had to make a

---

[1]Shares invested in such were usually preferred shares.

[2]<u>Genusscheine</u> are special rights to a share of profits or liquidation proceeds but have no nominal value.

special payment of one quarter of the nominal value of his shares (or see their value reduced to half their nominal value). In more concrete terms, this arrangement meant that Bethmann had to pay 250 marks per share on the large block of Sürther shares held by Bethmann on its own account and on Bethmann's part of the syndicate holdings.[1] Almost every shareholder made the required special payment, so that the plan brought in the additional capital that it was intended to. For a second time, Bethmann had been called upon to supply new funds in an effort to extricate the firm from its financial difficulties. At least the new composition of the supervisory board resulting from this second infusion of capital offered the hope of a happier outcome.

By the beginning of 1896, these financial arrangements were completed and the Sürther Maschinenfabrik appeared to be in much sounder condition. A 3 per cent dividend was paid for 1895 and the firm's prospects for the following year were even better. By the end of 1896, this improved situation prompted Oppenheim to attempt to stimulate interest in Sürther shares by purchasing them on his own account and "inspiring" favorable articles about the firm in the press. Oppenheim's efforts required the cooperation of his syndicate partners who assured him no sales would be made without his being informed in advance. Friction developed between Oppenheim and the two Frankfurt banks of the syndicate when the shares continued to be offered for sale on the Frankfurt market. Finally in May, 1897, after the firm declared a 5 1/2 per cent dividend

[1]On Bethmann's part of the syndicate holdings alone a payment of more than 10,000 marks was required.

and the Frankfurt bourse continued to show no interest in the shares, Oppenheim suggested that the syndicate be dissolved. In spite of the company's better showing and the then prevalent bull market, the syndicate had been unable to sell its remaining shares and was promptly dissolved.

Since the company was able to pay a dividend of 6 per cent in each of the three following boom years, Oppenheim attempted to create a broader market for the shares on his own. In July, 1897, he notified Bethmann of the very encouraging state of affairs in Sürth and asked his help in not disturbing efforts to make the best of this opportunity. Oppenheim had interested the Deutsche Effekten -und Wechselbank in promoting the shares among its clientele.[1] Bethmann was very enthusiastic about this possibility realizing that a bank of this type was more skilled in selling industrial securities. Whether anything came of this effort is not clear from the record. The last items in Bethmann's correspondence concern the firm's reduction of the nominal value of its shares by half in June, 1903. The firm's favorable turn did not continue beyond the depression that began in 1900 after which no dividends were paid. The Sürther Maschinenfabrik went into liquidation in 1908.

The story of Gebrüder Bethmann's role in this industrial share issue is striking not so much for what occurred as for what did not. At one point in his correspondence with Oppenheim, Bethmann wrote "we see our position in the Sürther business as solely that of an issuing bank."[2] Yet there was an immense difference between the manner in which

---

[1]The Deutsche Effekten- und Wechselbank was a relatively small <u>Kreditbank</u> located in Frankfurt am Main and founded in 1872.

[2]Copy of a letter signed only "Gebrüder Bethmann," Frankfurt am Main, February 8, 1892 (<u>Bethmann Archiv</u>, V, 568-569).

the major Kreditbanken functioned as issuing banks and that in which Bethmann did. Although a major shareholder, Bethmann did not accept a seat on the supervisory board of the firm. Furthermore, Bethmann never showed any concern for the technological side of the firm's operations and never showed itself capable of or interested in having them properly evaluated. Moreover, a member of Gebrüder Bethmann seems never to have gone to Sürth and Bethmann scarcely even communicated with the company. Plainly put, Bethmann did not have much of a relationship with the Sürther Maschinenfabrik. Its most notable service to the company was to furnish funds on two occasions when the company found itself in difficulty.

Evidently Bethmann's conception of the role of an issuing bank was rather narrow. Bethmann wished merely to sell securities, hold some on its own account for investment or future sale and leave relations with the company whose securities were being issued to the other banks involved. Such a stance is suitable if the aim is to mobilize capital for industrial investment opportunities that others have discovered and investigated. Many private banks functioned in this way, although excluding a select group, they rarely did so as issuing banks. In such a conception the daring and innovative side of banking is left to others. Had only banks cast in Bethmann's mold been called upon to perform the novel and risky tasks required in German industrialization, the German experience would have been quite different.

Yet the conclusion should not be drawn from these two conversions that Bethmann's experience with industrial firms was always in some way ill-fated. Gebrüder Bethmann had the capacity to learn to adjust to new circumstances however confusing or distasteful. The Bethmanns' adaptation to the new environment of industrial capitalism is illustrated by their involvement in the Chemisch-Elektrische Fabrik Prometheus, G.m.b.H. of Frankfurt.[1] The firm was a limited liability company formed by four local private banks and two commercial firms who were its partners of Gesellschafter. These banks were Gebrüder Bethman, von Erlanger & Sohne, Grunelius & Co. and D. & J. de Neufville and the firms were Hartmann & Braun and Voight & Häffner. The Prometheus company was created in April, 1896, in order to exploit various electrical heating element patents previously having belonged to Voight & Häffner. The patents were suitable for scientific, commercial and consumer applications but were intended primarily for consumer devices. While the company's efforts to exploit these patents did not proceed smoothly, they did end in success for the company's partners.

The Prometheus scheme was brought to Bethmann by de Neufville in March, 1896. The contract constituting the company called for a total initial investment by the partners of 150,000 marks of which Erlanger's share was the largest (40,000 marks), Hartmann and Braun's the smallest (10,000 marks). Bethmann's share was 25,000 marks and was to be paid in installments as needed as were the other shares. Provision was made in the contract for expanding the capital of the firm either by additional investments by the partners or by bringing in new partners. According to the contract, shares in the company had to be in units of at least 5,000 marks with each 100 marks invested entitling a partner to one vote.

---

[1] Bethmann Archiv, V, 278.

Most decisions were reached by simply majority vote. Meetings of the partners were held roughly every six months, often in the offices of one of the banks involved and extensive minutes were kept and reproduced for each partner. These thirty-three "protocols" give a detailed account of the development of the firm including decisions reached concerning commercial, financial and technological problems.

The extent to which the development of the Prometheus company was autonomous poses a difficult problem for despite its separate legal identity it was in practice an outgrowth of Voight and Häffner, an established and important Frankfurt electrical equipment firm. Messrs. Voight and Häffner were the original directors of Prometheus and the premises it occupied belonged to the Voight and Häffner firm. These circumstances strongly suggest that Voight and Häffner was seeking to branch out into a new field for which patents were at hand and capital was lacking or relatively expensive. By joining forces with a group of local investors, Voight and Häffner could obtain the needed capital and share the risks at a cost of merely sharing the profits. From this perspective, Prometheus appears more the special vehicle of Voight and Häffner than the common instrument of all the partners.

This view applies most directly to the technological aspects of Prometheus operations. Of the original partners only Voight and Häffner had the technical expertise to make technological decisions with confidence. In a special agreement (<u>Abshrift</u>) of October 22, 1896, the Deutsche Gold- und Silber-Scheide-Anstalt was permitted to join the company with a share of 10,000 marks. This action brought Dr. Heinrich Rössler, a director of Degussa and a figure well-informed in the technology of the chemical industry, into the group of partners. His technical competence served Prometheus well and the resources of his firm were also brought into play on occasion. The highly detailed technical comments of these men recorded in the minutes must have been an enlightening experience for the Bethmann partners and the other bankers in attendance whose contributions to Prometheus came in other fields.

What the bankers brought to Prometheus was considerable commercial acumen, an international network of financial contacts and, of course, the needed capital which could be augmented if they wished. The possibility that additional capital would be required was a very real one. Widespread financial contacts could be useful to Prometheus because in addition to the German patents for its products it held similar patents in France, Austria, Hungary, Italy, Belgium, and Switzerland and had applications pending in the United States, Sweden, Norway and later Russia. Commercial sophistication and contacts were of obvious value, not least in arranging for and evaluating dealers for the firm's products. In the light of these considerations it was likely that the banks would also contribute their share to the firm's success. The mix of abilities represented by the partners suggests that Bethmann's decision to participate in the Prometheus company was well-founded.

The first year and a half of the company's operations included the full range of problems that might have been expected to face a new firm. A patent dispute was resolved. Efforts were made to assist in solving the technical problems of Prometheus' supplier of porcelain products. Special very explicit instructions were sent to the firm supplying these articles so that they would be produced exactly to Prometheus' specifications.

While they were kept informed of these technical matters, the partners took the initiative in other fields. Bethmann's special contribution to Prometheus was to use its contacts in France to find a French company that would exploit its French patents. Bethmann began its efforts in France in January, 1897, and the arrangements with the French firm were completed by June. Valuable as such efforts were, they were overshadowed by Prometheus' requirements of a more tangible kind of assistance from the partners, capital.

After all of the original capital of the firm was paid over in October, 1897, discussions began about expanding its capital. Before increasing their investments, some of the partners wanted assurance about the profits that could be expected. The partners' committee comprised of all of the partners asked Rössler to make the required estimates. Calling upon Degussa's technical department, Rössler was able to provide a highly detailed analysis of Prometheus' costs and profit prospects. Appended to Rössler's letter of December 4, 1897, were four pages of painstaking calculations of all aspects of Prometheus' operations. Rössler concluded that the firm could ultimately be expected to earn about 16 per cent on an increased capital of 250,000 marks. Provided with Rössler's estimates, Bethmann and his fellow partners could make an informed decision about the capital expansion. In December, 1897, the partners agreed to provide Prometheus with an additional 80,000 marks.

Since financing a new firm involved difficulties and expenses that could not be foreseen even by the most precise calculations, lack of sufficient capital proved a recurring problem for Prometheus. The balance sheet as of December 31, 1897, showed a loss of 123,271 marks for the year and the following year's loss was 176,414 marks. These losses reflected production problems and experimentation with new products and were not unusual under the circumstances. At partners' meetings in 1898 and 1899 usually held in Bethmann's offices, the firm's problems were discussed at length. The minutes of these meetings indicate that the use of porcelain was never entirely satisfactory and that the firm had begun to experiment with mica as a substitute. Because demand for the firm's products was good and solutions to its problems were being actively pursued, the firm kept the confidence of the partners. They showed their confidence in May, 1899, by agreeing to a third increase of the firm's capital which amounted to 112,000 marks.

There were other reasons for the partners to be hopeful of a positive resolution of Prometheus' problems. In April, 1898, the company had signed an agreement with Siemens and Halske, the giant German electrical firm, to sell and to promote its products. The presige of Siemens and Halske must certainly have been helpful to Prometheus. The firm's affairs were going smoothly outside Germany as well. By 1900 sales or patent agreements had been signed with firms in France, Belgium, Britain and the United States and efforts were under way to find an affiliate in Austria. In addition to Bethmann's help in finding the firm's French affiliate, the central role of the banks in forming these connections is illustrated by the comments of Max Baer of Erlanger (at the meeting of June 25, 1900). Conditions were apparently very difficult in Austria and the firm had not been able to come to terms with a prospective affiliate in Vienna, the Schuckert works.[1] "Herr Baer confirmed these conditions and offered to

---

[1]The Schuckert works was a branch of the German Schuckert company, a major electrical firm which later merged with Siemens and Halske.

attempt to intervene in our [Prometheus'] favor on the basis of his close ties to the Austrian Länderbank presuming that the situation is at all suitable. . . ."[1] Nothing came of this proposal because Siemens bought the firm's Austrian and Hungarian patent rights in the following year. Although it is not possible to trace all the connections which led to Prometheus' foreign affiliations, it is clear from such examples that the banks were doing their job.

In spite of the fact that Prometheus' affairs showed promise, none of the partners had as yet realized any return on his investment. The losses of the first two years were followed by four more years of losses. In 1899 the company lost 167,963 marks, in 1900 166,953 marks, in 1901 96,801 marks and in 1902 6,025 marks. It was not until about eight years after the formation of Prometheus that any of its earnings were paid out as profits to the partners. If one assumes that a wait of this length was anticipated by the partners as the minutes of the meetings suggest, then the partners' investment represented ambitious risk-taking. The length of time required to be reasonably certain of a profitable outcome in the venture was somewhat shorter. The firm's accounts indicate that 1900 was the crucial year in this respect because in that year the firm began to earn sizable profits on sales of its products. Yet even six years of risk-taking with no return is impressive.

Any remaining doubts about Prometheus must have vanished by the end of 1903. Four per cent on its capital was paid to the partners in that

---

[1]Protokoll of June 25, 1900 (Bethmann Archiv, V, 278).

year and the firm's technical, marketing and patent exploitation problems were well in hand. Mica had been successfully substituted for porcelain in most of its products, eliminating its most serious technical problem. Most foreign licensees were doing well with the firm's patents thereby adding appreciably to its revenues. Furthermore, the firm's relations with Siemens-Schuckert were cemented on a highly advantageous basis.[1] The arrangement between Prometheus and Siemens-Schuckert provided that the latter sell the products of the former under the Siemens name and make no effort to develop similar products of its own. While the banks could claim no credit for helping to solve Prometheus' technical problems, the minutes of the partners' meeting of 1904 suggest that Max Baer of Erlanger was instrumental in getting the agreement with Siemens-Schuckert. Therefore at least part of Prometheus' success can be attributed to the activities of the banks on its behalf. The partners' willingness to risk sufficient capital was, of course, another cause of this success.

The subsequent history of Prometheus is of less interest in this context. The firm's fortunes continued to improve culminating in a 22 per cent dividend for the year 1910. The approach of these very favorable results led to discussions of an absorption of Prometheus by Voight and Häffner on the basis of an exchange of shares at a ratio slightly favoring the latter. After Prometheus' strong showing, the terms were altered and the exchange of shares was made on a one for one basis. These terms were quite favorable to the partners since they received shares

---

[1] Some of the operations of Siemens and Schuckert were combined beginning in 1903.

that were well-established on the Frankfurt bourse and were spared the costs of issue and promotion of new shares. The exchange of shares took place in May, 1911. The short but lucrative experience of Bethmann and his fellow partners had been satisfactory in every respect. Bethmann had gained handsome returns and also further experience with investment in industry.

Bethmann's direct experience with industrial finance was extremely limited in comparison with that of the major *Kreditbanken*, but Bethmann had a significant, if minor, indirect role in industrial finance. In many instances Bethmann acted as a participant in the syndicates of *Kreditbanken*. Three representative examples of securities issues by leading *Kreditbanken* in which Bethmann participated may be used to examine the relations of the private bank to the *Kreditbank* in the field of large scale industrial finance. Two of the three issues, that of the Elektrische Licht- und Kraftanlagen Aktien Gesellschaft and that of A. Goerz and Company, were made under the leadership of the Deutsche Bank and the third issue, that of the Serbian government, was arranged chiefly by Berliner Handelsgesellschaft. From Bethmann's point of view, the central decision to be made in such cases was whether or not to accept a syndicate participation that had been offered to his bank. This decision was made on the basis of the strength and prestige of the leading bank and the impression created by the material presented in support of the issue. Bethmann's shares in such syndicates were usually small and were sometimes arranged through local banks that acted as Frankfurt agents of the issuing *Kreditbank*. Once in such a syndicate, Bethmann played a relatively passive role, but even a passive role had its significance.

The first of these three syndicates in which Bethmann took part was the most routine. The Elektrische Licht- und Kraftanlagen Aktien Gesellschaft was an independent trust company organized by the Deutsche Bank for Siemens and Halske to finance the construction of its numerous, often foreign, electrical projects.[1] Boom conditions in the highly capital intensive electrical industry in the second half of the 1890's caused it to seek new sources of capital and, in the case of Siemens, led to the formation of the new trust company. The new company was established in December, 1897, with a total share capital of 30 million marks divided into two series of 15 million marks each. The full amount of the capital of the first series had to be paid in almost immediately while only one quarter of the capital of the second series was paid in so that the actual paid in capital of the company was 18,750,000 marks. When the issue of these shares was announced, notice was also given that 30 million marks of bonds would also be issued at some future date.

Of this unusually large issue Bethmann's part was 50,000 marks of shares and an equal amount of bonds. This participation was arranged through Jacob S. H. Stern who was a senior member of the syndicate organized by the Deutsche Bank. Apparently Bethmann found his participation rather large and half was immediately offered to the Bank in Zürich. The Swiss accepted so that Bethmann took only half of his quota from Stern on his own account. The several steps from the Deutsche Bank to Stern to Bethmann to the Bank in Zürich illustrate the complexity of the network of banks that allowed industrial capital to be raised and risk to be broadly

---

[1] Bethmann Archiv, V, 916.

distributed. Bethmann's place was nearer the bottom than the top of this network for securities issue; accordingly Bethmann had little influence on the affairs of the network as a whole.

Reflecting this relative passivity, Bethmann made few decisions of any consequence. In March, 1898, he merely chose not to increase his share in the syndicate when additional shares were offered indicating a desire to confine his commitment to the shares already accepted. Decisions concerning the entire syndicate were made by the leading banks of the syndicate in Berlin. They decided on the price at which the fully paid in series of the shares were issued at the Berlin bourse, kept the records and distributed the profits. In October, 1898, Bethmann received about 3,500 marks as his share of the profits on this series. Thereafter, Bethmann merely read the syndicate reports and collected dividends on his investment. Bethmann must have been satisfied with his participation because in 1904 he bought back at a premium half of the shares he had sold to the Swiss. A novel investment vehicle, the trust company, allowed Bethmann to share in Siemens' prosperity without having any direct relationship to Siemens whatever.

In addition to the advantages of this arrangement there was one serious disadvantage. The shares that Bethmann held in the only partly paid in series could not be sold on the most advantageous basis because they had not been admitted to any bourse.[1] It was not until 1910 that the leading banks of the syndicate chose to bring this second series of

---

[1] Admittance to exchanges was in effect a part of the value of shares traded on exchanges. Other things being equal shares not admitted would be traded at a discount.

shares on the market and the manner of their doing so is quite revealing. In August, 1910, a confidential letter from the Deutsche Bank informed Bethmann that full payment on the shares would soon be requested. Thereafter the Deutsche Bank was organizing a _Verkaufsgemeinschaft_ (selling group) under its leadership "if all or most owners of the shares wanted to bind themselves in a common management of the market." The key feature of this arrangement was the pledge of each owner not to sell shares independently. The agreement provided for the formation of a "syndicate for market regulation" in which each member could participate in the sales with an equal quota (i.e., an equal percentage of his total holdings). For those who accepted, the agreement transferred the burden of selling the shares and of making all decisions such sales required to the Deutsche Bank.

Bethmann accepted this offer and joined the group as did 93 per cent of all shareholders. The Deutsche Bank sold shares in three blocks of varying sizes between November, 1910, and May, 1911. Before the sale of each block, members of the group were asked what part of their holdings they wished to include and were informed in the second and third rounds of sales what what the minimum price would be. By arranging sales in this way, the Deutsche Bank served Bethmann and the other syndicate subscribers very well. Profits received by the subscribers computed as returns on the amounts invested were 26 per cent, 41 per cent and 46 per cent on each block respectively or 37 per cent on the total sales. Such profits were more than generous in view of the quite limited risk that this investment entailed. Results of this kind obtained almost entirely through efforts and iniative of the Deutsche Bank make it easy to understand why Bethmann so eagerly participated in the syndicate organized by the major *Kreditbanken*.

Several years before joining the Siemens trust company syndicate Bethmann had participated in another large syndicate led by the Deutsche Bank. The record of Bethmann's participation in this second syndicate bears examination chiefly because of its international aspects. At the beginning of 1893, the Deutsche Bank realized its plans for the creation of a South African gold mining company. Acting in cooperation with the Berliner Handelgesellschaft and Jacob S. H. Stern, the Deutsche Bank chose Adolf Goerz, an experienced figure in South African mining, to head the new venture. The firm was called A. Goerz and Company and was organized under German law but had its principal office in Johannesburg.[1] The firm's founding was unusual in that the Goerz company had not only a founding capital of 3,200,000 marks but also a "special payment obligation" (*Nachschussverpflichtung*) of an equal amount of which the shareholders could be called upon to pay a part or the entire sum. By the standards of the day, the organization of so large an enterprise was a major undertaking.

Although the record is not clear on this point, it was presumably Stern that interested Bethmann in the syndicate. In any case the Deutsche Bank contacted Bethmann in January, 1893, gave formal notice of the terms of the project and offered Bethmann a participation of 25,000 marks with an equal special obligation. Favorably impressed, Bethmann accepted and

[1] *Bethmann Archiv*, V, 222.

paid in his share of the capital in the same month. Before the year's end, Bethmann was also asked to pay in half of the amount of the special obligation which was requested and then paid back to Bethmann in varying amounts during the course of the syndicate's operations. No dividend was paid for its first year although the firm appeared to be progressing in a satisfactory way. The Goerz annual report for 1893 discusses its operations and prospects and analyzes its investment portfolio in detail. Such reports informed Bethmann not only of Goerz affairs but of South African affairs in general.

That Bethmann had at least one other South African investment which made such information useful was shown by a letter of mid-1894 from A. Goerz and Company.[1] Goerz has a large interest in the Princess Estate and Gold Mining Company, a firm which was shortly to consider a capital expansion at a special general meeting. Bethmann was asked by Goerz to contact various shareholders to urge them to support a planned capital expansion and to gather their proxies. Bethmann was happy to oblige. Its cooperation shows that the members of a syndicate could on occasion be most helpful to its leadership in functions other than the mere provision of capital. The membership of a syndicate constituted a reservoir of support in matters like proxy dispute as well as a pool to share the risk of a given investment.

With the exception of its role in gathering support for the Deutsche Bank in this instance, Bethmann played as passive a role in this syndicate as it did in the one previously examined. The two syndicates were also similar in that both were quite profitable. The dividends on Goerz shares

[1]The letter is signed by Max Steinthal, who was a leading figure of the Deutsche Bank but was written in his capacity as a director of Goerz.

for 1894 and 1895 were 35 per cent and 50 per cent respectively, indicating that Bethmann recovered much of its investment in that period alone. When in 1897 the Goerz company doubled its capital and Bethmann was offered a share equal to its original share, Bethmann accepted quickly. Later in the same year, the Deutsche Bank informed Bethmann of a plan to transform A. Goerz and Company into a South African corporation. This change was to be accomplished in cooperation with the German banks involved and the Union Bank of London, the Banque de Paris et des Pays-Bas, the Crédit Lyonnais, the Nationale Bank der Südafrikanischen Republik and the Standard Bank of South Africa. The plan was soon accepted and Bethmann through his membership in the syndicate found himself involved in a quite sizable financial project.

Until the approval of the plan, Bethmann and the other shareholders were not able to sell their shares. The aim of the plan was to create a broad international market for Goerz shares and to help the syndicate members to realize their investment. By incorporating under South African law, the Goerz company could issue one pound (20 mark) shares and avoid the 1,000 mark per share minimum imposed by German law. This far lower par value greatly facilitated sale of shares in London and Paris where they were introduced on the exchanges. As in the previously discussed syndicate a special group was organized to manage sales of the shares. Bethmann put one quarter of his shares at the disposal of the group in 1898 and they were sold by 1899 at a profit to Bethmann of 62 1/2 per cent. It is likely that Bethmann would have been able to sell the remainder of his shares on even better terms had the Boer War not intervened. Although Bethmann's connection with the Goerz syndicate continued until

1909, this continuing connection need not be traced for present purposes. It is sufficient to note that Bethmann's participation in these syndicates brought high profits relative to the risk that had to be borne and involved little autonomous action on Bethmann's part.

These syndicates differ in many respects from the third syndicate under consideration. The Serbian State Loan of 1909 was as its name indicates not an industrial securities issue but rather a Serbian government bond issue organized and conducted by a group of French and German banks acting in concert.[1] Why should such a loan be included in a discussion of Bethmann's relations to industry and to other banks serving industry? The answer is that this loan represented another type of bank service to German industry, the indirect financing of German industrial exports. It was common knowledge in 1909 that the Serbian government sought these funds to make purchases of arms and railroad equipment.[2] Where the orders for this material would be placed was a matter of some interest to German industrialists and bankers.

The German banker most experiences in financial dealings with Serbia was Carl Fürstenberg of the Berliner Handelsgesellschaft. Because of Germany's close attachment to Austria-Hungary, Serbia's principal antagonist during this period of political turbulence in the Balkans, the French had displaced the Germans as the favored lenders in Belgrade. Although a group of French banks had won the lion's share of this bond

---

[1] Bethmann Archiv, V, 914.

[2] Letter of Carl Borgnis, Frankfurt am Main, June 30, 1909 (Bethmann Archiv, V, 914).

issue, they chose for unknown reasons to include Carl Fürstenberg. He agreed to enter the negotiations which were apparently well under way by mid-1909 when his correspondence with Bethmann about the Serbian loan began. Just how the two banks came together for this issue is not clear from the record. The exchange of letters of June and July, 1909, merely suggests that Bethmann's participation was already projected at this point.

In a letter of July 1, 1909, to Carl Borgnis, a partner in Gebrüder Bethmann, Fürstenberg noted that a meeting had been scheduled for July 5 in Frankfurt to decide the question of his participation and that "I cannot decide whether an association with Mr. Naville [of the Société Financière d'Orient of Paris] or with the Serbian authorities is more loathsome to me." As a notorious wit and a veteran of many such bond issues, Fürstenberg was urging Bethmann not to expect an affair of this sort to proceed smoothly. The meeting took place as scheduled between Fürstenberg, Borgnis and a representative of the French group named Noel Bardac. After the conversations, a long memorandum listing the conditions to which the French and the Germans had agreed was prepared and released to the press.

According to the memorandum, the Serbian government required about 110 million francs (88 million marks) of which the German banks were to provide one third. The German and French banks were to conduct the issue under a common contract but to keep separate accounts for the respective bank groups although a common price was to be agreed on. Furthermore, it was expressly agreed that the funds raised for the Serbian government by the German group were to be held and dispensed by the Berliner Handelsgesellschaft and were to be used only to pay for materials ordered from German manufacturers. The material to be ordered in Germany was specified. All that was needed was the approval of the French and Serbian governments and Fürstenberg declared himself ready to go to Paris to negotiate a final agreement. Of special interest to Bethmann was its mention in the memorandum as a leading bank of the German group that would represent Frankfurt.

Approval from the governments was readily obtained and the final negotiations were put off until autumn. Discussions resumed in November, 1909, and a provisional contract was soon agreed upon. The total amount of the loan was raised to 150 million francs but the German share remained the same, 37.5 million francs (30 million marks) or one quarter of the new total. In a letter to Bethmann, Fürstenberg described the satisfactory manner in which the talks were progressing and commented:

> . . . it is of exceptional importance that we hear clearly from the Serbian government what minimum amount of the loan will be spent in Germany. Furthermore, this minimum amount must remain in the hands of the Berliner Handelsgesellschaft for the purpose of paying suppliers. Although this condition is self-explanatory, it is not clear that the Serbs will not cause difficulties for some absurd reason. In that case we would go home and refuse further cooperation.[1]

In a later letter written after the signing of the preliminary protocol, Fürstenberg mentioned to Bethmann that he had reserved the right of withdrawal in the event that the Serbian government did not provide him

---

[1]Letter of Carl Fürstenberg, Geschäftsinhaber (limited partner) of the Berliner Handelsgesellschaft, Berlin, November 1, 1909 (*Bethmann Archiv*, V, 914).

or the German ambassador in Belgrade with a clear declaration about the orders for German industry.[1]

After the signing of the preliminary protocol, preparations for the bond issue proceeded well and soon appeared virtually complete. The bonds were taken over from the Serbian government at a price of 84 1/2 per cent and separate issues were planned for Paris and Berlin. Only the approval of the Serbian parliament had yet to be obtained. Within the German group arrangements were also settled easily. Bethmann took 8 per cent of the German share or 2,765,000 francs (about 2,200,000 marks) which was quite a large participation by Bethmann's standards. The size of Bethmann's share is accounted for by its place as an issuing bank in the German group with an exclusive right of issue in Frankfurt. The bonds were much in demand and Bethmann's Unterbeteiligte (those taking part in the syndicate under Bethmann) included such leading names as Jacob S. H. Stern, Lazard-Speyer-Ellissen, J. Dreyfus, Veit L. Homberger and even Delbrück, Leo and Co. (a Berlin bank to which Bethmann was technically not permitted to allot shares).[2] A successful issue seemed assured before December 31, 1909, when the banks' commitment to make the issue expired.

The financial press reflected the optimism asserting that the loan was completely settled and that Krupp had been assured large contracts

---

[1] Letter of Carl Fürstenberg, Berlin, November 7, 1909 (Bethmann Archiv, V, 914).

[2] These shares were allotted by special agreement with the Berliner Handelsgesellschaft.

from the German banks' share.[1] To Bethmann's surprise December 31 passed and no issue was made. In a very revealing personal note, Fürstenberg explained the situation. Because of disagreement about the division of contracts for war material, the banks' deadline was extended until January 12, 1910. Quite irritated, Fürstenberg remarked:

> In these discussions it has been possible to get an impression of the enormous extra charges which Schneider [Creusot] must include to satisfy Mr. Naville and associates. One may judge from this the enormous sums that they have swindled us out of. What fine people.[2]

In a somewhat later letter, Fürstenberg provided a full explanation of his view of the situation. The prices asked by the French for their arms were far higher than those asked by Krupp. Furthermore, the quality of the French arms was regarded as far inferior to that of the German. These were factors that the Serbian government could not entirely ignore. On the other hand, the French demanded the greater share of the orders and the approval of the French government depended upon its being given. Fürstenberg found himself in a no less delicate position since, as he explained:

> We have won the support of the foreign office and the German ambassador in Belgrade for this loan after we gave assurances that the proceeds of the German part would be spent entirely or almost entirely in Germany. For this reason our difficulties are even more serious because we can hardly place a loan in

---

[1] Hamburger Handels- und Borsenblatt, November 26, 1909.

[2] Note of Carl Fürstenberg, Berlin, January 2, 1910 (<u>Bethmann Archiv</u>, V, 914).

> Germany for the benefit of the French arms industry. The ministerial council in Belgrade deliberates all day long without coming to any conclusion.[1]

In fact, it was not until the middle of February that the difficulties could be resolved to the satisfaction of all parties.

The formalities were completed quickly and the issue took place on February 15, 1910. The Serbian loan was a resounding success. The bonds sold very well in Germany and their price rose on the exchange without the intervention of the issuing syndicate. Fürstenberg must have been pleased with the happy outcome from which not only his bank but also the German firms receiving contracts stood to benefit. Bethmann was pleased as well both with the success of the Serbian loan and with its role in mobilizing the resources of Frankfurt in support of it. In this issue as in the others of this type that have been discussed, Bethmann's role was passive and involved little influence on the policy or conduct of the syndicate beyond the local level.

Bethmann's experience in these six cases provides the basis for answers to the questions about the private banks that were raised at the outset. What was the role of the private bank in the years 1870 to 1914? The evidence suggests that the private bank did not engage in aggressive, independent investment banking in the service of industry.[2] The traditional practice of commercial banking and the financing of state debt continued to be the chief functions of Bethmann. Independent investment banking on

---

[1]Letter of Carl Fürstenberg, Berlin, January 11, 1910 (Bethmann Archiv, V, 914).

[2]There are notable exceptions in the Rhineland and among the larger private banks of Berlin.

behalf of industry was rare and, when practised, was conducted in a hesitant and limited fashion. Bethmann's involvement in the Deutsche Verlagsanstalt, the Sürther Maschinenfabrik, and the Chemisch- Elektrische Fabrik Prometheus reflect the very narrow bounds within which Bethmann's independent industrial investment banking took place. Had the capital for German industrialization came solely from such sources, there is reason to believe that its character and timing would have been most unlike what the record shows.

The characteristics of German industrialization derive in no small part from the provision of capital to German industry by *Kreditbanken* as well as private banks. Moreover the private banks appear to have served industry more effectively as agents of the *Kreditbanken* than as independent actors in the field of investment banking. The relationship between private banks and *Kreditbanken* is well illustrated by Bethmann's participation in the syndicates for the Elektrische Licht- und Kraftanlagen, A. G., A. Goerz and Company and the Serbian State Loan of 1909. This cooperative relationship allowed the capital of the private banks to be mustered easily and routinely in support of the major industrial promotions of the *Kreditbanken*. Although clearly subordinate to the *Kreditbanken* in these syndicates, the private banks performed services in securities issue and distribution the value of which should be fairly acknowledged.

The character of relations between private banks and *Kreditbanken* suggests one last troublesome question regarding the former. To what extent did private banks change and adapt to new conditions in this period and what was the meaning of any such changes? To deny that Gebrüder Bethmann changed considerably would be to ignore a subtle evolution. In 1870 Bethmann did not participate significantly in industrial finance and appears to have regarded it with suspicion and perhaps also disdain. In discrete stages Bethmann's attitude changed. First came the Deutsche Verlagsanstalt conversion in which Bethmann tried its hand, enjoyed a resounding success and gained confidence for similar ventures in the future. This conversion also reveals that a fear of isolation from new opportunities was a consideration that Bethmann was beginning to take into account.

Bethmann showed greater reluctance to take technological considerations into account. The record of Bethmann's financing of the Sürther Maschinenfabrik shows the risks of neglecting so basic an aspect of industrial finance. While no direct connection can be found between this participation and Bethmann's role in the Chemisch- Elektrische Fabrik Prometheus, the contrast between the two cases suggests that Bethmann put to work in the latter what was learned in the former. Learning that technological collaborators in an industrial investment had to be competent was an expensive but necessary lesson. The competence of Voight and Häffner could be attested to by the personal knowledge of the partners. How much familiarity with technology the Bethmann partners themselves gained is not clear from the record. Since technological sophistication had come to depend increasingly on specialized technical training in these years, this aspect of Bethmann's experience should not be overemphasized. Yet Bethmann had come to show a greater understanding of the problems of industrial finance and a greater willingness to involve himself in such ventures.

Because the extent of the changes described above is considerable, the pace at which they occured was relatively slow. Relative to the rapid advance of German industry in the pre-First World era, the rate at which Bethmann adjusted to an industrial economy is not very striking. The proud Frankfurt patriciate of which the Bethmann partners were prominent members found its distaste for industry difficult to outgrow. Outgrowing this traditional outlook was in large measure a feature of that generational change that can be glimpsed in the correspondence of Moritz and Hugo von Bethmann or in the contrast between Franz Borgniz, who avoided industrial finance, and his son Carl, who conducted much of Bethmann's involvement with industry. It appears that it fell to the sons to make a transition that could not be made by the fathers.

Significant as this transition was for Bethmann, it would be misleading to overlook its limits. During the 1870's and most of the 1880's while Bethmann's general policy remained avoidance of industrial finance, the newer members of the circle of the major _Kreditbanken_ established themselves basing much of their power on the field of finance that Bethmann shunned. Gebrüder Bethmann remained a partnership with limited capital and a traditional outlook. There could never have been any question of Bethmann's emulating his larger corporate colleagues. Instead Gebrüder Bethmann chose a path that enabled it to preserve its character and at the same time to adjust to an increasingly industrialized economy. Bethmann participated in industrial finance as a member of the syndicates of _Kreditbanken_ when the projects being financed appeared sound and profitable. In this way, while remaining independent, Bethmann often functioned as an agent of the major _Kreditbanken_. This compromise was a satisfactory one for all parties concerned and offered an agreeable *modus vivendi* for those private banks strong enough to remain independent. To many other private banks the continuing march of industrialization meant absorption or liquidation.

CHAPTER III

THE KREDITBANK - THE DEUTSCHE BANK

The development of major Kreditbanken has been outlined in Chapter I. It bears repearting that virtually all of the literature dealing with these banks emphasizes their contribution to German economic growth in the era of industrialization. The central place within this literature belongs to Jacob Riesser's Zur Entwicklungsgeschichte der deutschen Grossbanken mit besonderer Rücksicht auf die Konzentrationsbestrebungen.[1] This work remains to this day the only comprehensive work of real merit devoted to the Kreditbanken. Since Professor Riesser was also a manager and director of the Darmstadter Bank and had free access to its archives, his work has almost the quality of an original source.[2] In 1905 he wrote:

> . . . the intimate relations [of industrial firms] with the large banks and their extensive resources served as a new stimulus for various industrial establishments to extend their operations and influence in their respective districts, to establish more firmly their position as against other establishments, groups, and particularly cartels, as well as within cartels, by way of combinations, consolidations, and fusions of all sorts. In this way concentration in banking, which had been

---

[1]Jacob Riesser, Zur Entwicklungsgeschichte der deutschen Grossbanken mit besonderer Rücksicht auf die Konzentrationsbestrebungen (Jena: Verlag von Gustav Fischer, 1906).

[2]Rondo E. Cameron, "Founding the Bank of Darmstadt," Explorations in Entrepreneurial History, VIII, No. 3 (1956), 113-130.

> greatly influenced both in the extent and rapidity of its progress by developments in industry, and particularly by the formation of cartels, in turn helped to bring about concentration in industry.[1]

This emphasis upon the interdependency of the development of banking and that of industry became his central theme. It is largely to the force of this interpretation that the Kreditbanken owe their proud reputation among past and present scholars. The essential elements of Riesser's interpretation have not only gone unchallenged; they have been supported powerfully and often.

Comparable to Riesser's work in quality, although not in scope, is Otto Jeidels' Das Verhältnis der deutschen Grossbanken zur Industrie mit besonderer Berücksichtigung der Eisenindustrie.[2] Jeidels analyzes the interdependency of banks and industry in German economic development from a perspective whose essentials do not differ from that of Riesser. The fact that Jeidels limits his work to only the largest Kreditbanken and the coal, metallurgical and electrical industries gives his study an even sharper focus than that of Riesser. The issue of vertical, and to a lesser extent, horizontal integration in industry and its relation to bank industrial policy figures heavily in both works. Both Riesser and Jeidels stress the interconnection of the merger movement within banking and that within heavy industry, a problem that will be given

---

[1] Riesser (English edition), pp. 617-618.

[2] Otto Jeidels, "Das Verhältnis der deutschen Grossbanken zur Industrie mit besonderer Berücksichtigung der Eisenindustrie," in Staats- und sozialwissenschaftliche Forschungen, XXIV, Heft II (1905), 271.

some attention later in this discussion. Supplemented by Jeidels' work, the Riesser interpretation becomes even more formidable, so that it is not surprising that subsequent work by non-socialist scholars like Schulze-Gaevernitz, Karnath and Gehr remains broadly within Riesser's framework.[1]

This interpretation appears equally congenial to scholarship in the Marxian tradition. Marx himself noted the success of institutions in the Crédit Mobilier pattern in Prussia during the 1850's. "If Prussia cannot boast of an Issac Péreire, yet it possesses hundreds of Mevissens at the head of more Credit-mobiliers than the German Confederation has princes," Marx wrote in Preussen und die Hohenzollern um die Jahreswende, 1858-59.[2] In Kapital, the Crédit Mobilier idea was given only one brief mention, but these references suffice to indicate some interest on the part of Marx and Engels in this new institution.[3] Subsequent scholars of this school have been far more generous in the attention they give to Kreditbanken and their role in German industrial development. Among the best known Marxians to examine this problem was Rudolf Hilferding, whose Finanzkapital dwells at length on the significance of these banks.[4]

---

[1] Kurt Karnath, "Über die Stelling der Kreditbanken zur Industrie" (Ph.D. dissertation, University of Frankfurt, 1924). Martin Gehr, "Das Verhältnis zwischen Banken und Industrie in Deutschland seit der Mitte des 19. Jahrhunderts bis zur Bankendrise von 1931 unter besonderer Berücksichtigung des industriellen Grosskredits" (Ph.D. dissertation, University of Tübingen, 1959). Schulze-Gaevernitz, Die deutsche Kreditbank.

[2] Karl Marx, "Preussen und die Hohenzollern um die Jahreswende, 1858-59," in Marx-Engels-Lenin-Stalin--Zur deutschen Geschichte (Berlin: Akademic-Verlag, 1954).

[3] Karl Marx, Capital, III (Chicago: Charles H. Kerr & Co., 1909), 714.

[4] Rudolf Hilferding, Das Finanzkapital (Frankfurt: Europäische Verlaganstalt, 1968), p. 310 ff.

More recent Marxian scholarship in this field, like that of Blumberg, continues to reflect the same views.[1]

Such apparent unanimity among scholars of different schools and generations could be most embarassing. Are the problems concerning the role of the *Kreditbanken* in German economic development settled to the satisfaction of all? Obviously, they are not. What is generally accepted is that the *Kreditbanken* were able to influence heavily the course of German development and that they did so. This convenient consensus is one upon which this discussion is based. A full examination and substantiation of this view based on archival materials is too large a task for present purposes. In a broader sense this view of the banks will be assumed, and an effort will be made to examine and support it only with respect to the activities of one *Kreditbank* in one industry. In order to obtain the maximum benefit from this effort, the questions raised about the role of the *Kreditbanken* must be defined with care.

Two sorts of questions will be explored in order to determine the capacity of the banks to carry out an industrial policy. Questions which make clear the character of bank relations to industry comprise one category. What were the powers and responsibilities of the bankers? What ends did they pursue and how successful were their efforts? What tensions characterized these relations?

---

[1] Horst Blumberg, "Die Finanzierung der Neugrundungen und Erweiterungen von Industriebetrieben in Form der Aktiengesellschaften während der fünfziger Jahre des 19. Jahrhunderts in Deutschland, am Beispiel der preussischen Verhaltnisse erläutert" in Hans Mottek (ed.), *Studien zur Geschichte der Industriellen Revolution in Deutschland* (Berlin: Akademie-Verlag, 1960), pp. 200-206.

A second category of questions includes various aspects of *Kreditbank* relations to other *Kreditbanken* and, to a lesser extent, other prominent banks (for the most part, Berlin private banks). How did bankers function as a community? What was the character of their relations to each other? How were these relations conditioned by the environment in which they were operating? Both of these questions can be addressed on the basis of available material.

A third category of questions, those involving bank and industry relations with the state, is beyond the scope of the present inquiry because the necessary archival material is inaccessible or unavailable, and such questions will be touched upon only briefly. There is, of course, a large literature devoted to the problem of the role of the state in German industrialization. This literature is too large and wide-ranging even to summarize here.[1] All that is required for a useful inquiry into the role of the *Kreditbanken* in German economic development from 1870 to 1914 is the assumption that the state was actively concerned with such routine political matters as defense and the balance of trade.

In order to understand better the environment in which these banks and industrial firms were operating, the second category of questions, *Kreditbank* relations to other *Kreditbanken*, will be examined first. The most salient feature of the market in which the largest *Kreditbanken* operated was its oligopolistic character. The highest level in the hierarchy of German corporate banking was occupied by six banks. These

---

[1]This literature is surveyed in Richard Tilly, "Soll und Haben: Recent German Economic History and the Problem of Economic Development," *Journal of Economic History*, XXIX (June, 1969), 298.

banks provided most of the financial services to the major German industrial firms. The actions of any one of these banks would most likely affect those of the others. On the other hand, actions of smaller banks would not be likely to have any effect on the dealings of these leading _Kreditbanken_ with their major industrial accounts. The market structure implied here is one of oligopolistic competition. German bankers were acutely aware of this market structure, and this awareness is reflected in their correspondence. In a letter regarding the size of the quota of Delbrück, Leo and Company in a bond issue of Siemens and Halske, a director of the Deutsche Bank remarked that:

> . . . the influence of the firm [Delbrück, Leo and Co.] in important deals generally as well as that in the promotion of your bonds should not be estimated as very great and in any case cannot be regarded as equal to the influence of the Disconto-Gesellschaft, the Berliner Handelsgesellschaft and the other main participants.[1]

There will be occasion to return to this bond issue. For the moment this correspondence illustrates well the distinction between those banks that could compete at this level and those that could not.

Competition within this inner circle of six _Kreditbanken_ to provide financial services to German "big business" was very spirited. The origins of such competition may be sought in the structure of these banks. By the decade of the 1890's, all of these banks had built up very large amounts of share capital and reserves. Increasingly share capital and reserves on so large a scale were becoming necessary conditions for

---

[1] Letter from A. Gwinner to Dr. Bödiker, 1 April 1898. Note that letters cited in Chapter III are privately held.

providing banking services to the larger German industrial firms. The very magnitude of these capital resources impelled the six banks of this inner circle to seek accounts that could make large scale use of bank credit, since it was administratively easier to put these funds to profitable use serving large firms than small ones. For this reason, competition among these banks had two distinctive aspects: a quest for large industrial accounts, and an effort to increase the number of a bank's branches in various parts of Germany in order to be able to provide more geographically comprehensive service. The services provided by one of the major Kreditbanken did not differ very much from those offered by the other banks of the inner circle. Only with respect to regional emphasis were there significant differences. Since the Berliner Handelsgesellschaft had no branches outside Berlin , it could offer no regional representation at all. Other of these banks had stronger bases in some regions than others, a familiar case having been the well-established position of the Schaafhausen'scher Bankverein in the Rhineland.

As has been noted earlier, a quite extensive merger movement occurred within German banking between 1870 and 1913. The major Kreditbanken were the keenest competitors in the scramble to absorb or arrange suitable ties with lucrative regional banks. For the five major Kreditbanken that established regional branches or ties of some sort, Riesser gives the following figures as of 1908: branches--241; agencies--325; commandites--18; deposit offices--102; private banking houses absorbed--89; banks absorbed--43; and communities of interest by ownership or exchange of stock--16.[1] This movement toward integration in banking was also reflected

[1]Riesser (English edition), p. 1012. Note that a commandite is a partnership in which at least one partner has unlimited liability but other partners (often "silent" or secret partners) have limited liability. A

within the inner circle of the six largest Kreditbanken in 1902 when a community of interest agreement was signed by the Dresdner Bank and the Schaafhausen'scher Bankverein. Of course, steps toward integration at this level tended to reduce competition among Kreditbanken.

The competition to provide banking services to larger industrial firms was a more subtle affair. It was considered bad manners to make an aggressive effort to detach an industrial firm from a banking connection where a harmonious relationship existed; but, when a falling out occurred, the road lay open to competing banks. In the intricate politics of banking the relations of other banks with their major industrial accounts were matters bankers treated with discretion. Often mere off-hand remarks provide the best clues to the nature of this competition. In a letter commenting on the failure of a merger between two electrical firms, Georg Siemens, for many years the dominant figure in the management of the Deutsche Bank, wrote: "I was happy to hear that Löwe and A.E.G. are not merging, but that they are both staying with the Ber. H. G. [Berliner Handelsgesellschaft] is hopefully only a provisional arrangement [Provisorium]."[1] Had a competitor established so powerful a position in the electrical industry, Georg Siemens could not have accepted such a turn of events with equanimity.

The vigorous competition in which these banks were engaged did not prevent them from cooperating when their interests required it. The most

---

community of interest is an arrangement that allows two legally separate firms to operate in common in a clearly defined field.

[1] Letter from Georg Siemens in Genoa to the Deutsche Bank in Berlin, 17 January 1897.

common form of cooperation was the securities consortium. Since the development of the German heavy industrial sector was highly capital intensive, the magnitude of individual securities flotations was routinely greater than that which could be managed by one bank. The dynamics of such consortia have already been discussed with respect to the relations of smaller private banks to major Kreditbanken. Among the leading banks of a consortium, other considerations arose of which the most important was the size of a bank's quota. The size of a bank's quota was a measure of that bank's prestige and strength and the badge of the strongest was a full share. Getting a full share implied being able to sell it on terms specified by the consortium and to retain what could not be sold in the short run until such time as it could be sold. The successful functioning of a consortium depended upon the observation of its rules by all members. For example, underselling the consortium, if attempted by a large member, would ruin the market for the securities being promoted. Under these circumstances, the premium on cooperation was high.

A second mode of cooperation among banks was the coordination of policies towards industrial organization. While it goes too far to say that the banks were always and under all circumstances strong supporters of cartels or other schemes to organize markets, there are cases so clear as to leave little doubt of bank policy and of its influence. In coal and metallurgy, the banks are generally conceded to have played a vigorous role in promoting cartels. From the banks' point of view, such a policy favored not only the interest of these industries but their own interests as well. One of the most momentous cases of cartel organization was the formation of the Steel Works' Union in 1904. A crucial step in its organization was the inclusion of the Phoenix metallurgical firm, whose management opposed and resisted entry into the cartel. What followed was an open battle that provided a rare glimpse into the mechanics of bank influence in such cases. Riesser gives a perceptive account of the "Phoenix case":

> The management of the Phoenix was unwilling to enter the Steel Works' Union--which could not be organized without it--unless it received greater advantages than the union felt able to grant. There is little doubt that these efforts on behalf of the cartel were started by the banks which were not represented on the directorate of the Phoenix and which were therefore entirely free in their action. We may also grant that those firms which were represented on the board, as they asserted, refrained from exerting a direct influence on their customers as to how they should vote at the special meeting of stockholders of April 26, 1904, at which final action was to be taken. On the other hand, it is equally true that they maintained an attitude of "benevolent neutrality" toward the wishes for the realization of the Steel Works' Union.
>
> A benevolent neutrality of this kind was maintained on similar occasions also by banking establishments which counted among their clients' concerns, whose interests lay in the opposite direction. In business, as in politics, such an attitude may be of great importance. Under given circumstances it may be equivalent to the advancement of the cartel.[1]

The point of Riesser's subtle phrasing is that the failure of a bank to support a firm it served in a conflict like that involving the Phoenix firm was tantamount to supporting the firm's opponents. In an industrial

---

[1]Riesser (English edition), p. 727.

economy as large and highly developed as that of Germany, the effectiveness of the banks' industrial policy depended on close cooperation among individual banks and at least a passive acceptance of a given policy by them.

Beyond these specific fields of cooperation among bankers, there existed a common outlook consisting of views about their role and the roles of industry and government in the economy. Sharing such views vested in bankers a potential for cooperation which proved surprisingly strong when translated into action. The views of which the bankers' outlook was comprised are usually labelled "liberal ideology." Given the strength of the traditional role of the state in Prussia, the force of such liberal views, especially vis-a-vis the state, cannot be taken for granted. It is of more than passing interest that it took a challenge to one of the most basic canons of the liberal faith--private ownership of capital--to bring about a vigorous, unified response from the banking community. This response came in the celebrated Hibernia "battle" of 1904.

Government acquisition of the German railway network had caused some uneasiness among bankers and industrialists, so that when the Prussian treasury secretly acquired a large block of shares in the Hibernia, a firm that held some of the best bituminous coal land in Westphalia, the bankers prepared for a fight. The alarm was sounded by Carl Fürstenberg, who was the principal financial advisor to the Hibernia by virtue of his position in the Berliner Handelsgesellschaft. According to his account, Fürstenberg feared that "after all that had taken place in recent years [1880's and 1890's] there may have been a desire to oppose the admittedly real danger of private monopoly with state monopoly.[1] After commenting upon the contemporary conflict between the Kathedersozialisten and industrial leaders, he remarked that he quickly came to the conclusion that a "decisive battle" would be fought over the firm.[2] As soon as information of the treasury's action reached him, the battle was joined.

To foil the treasury's plan, Fürstenberg built up a united front of bank and industrial interests. Emil Kirdorf was his principal ally among the industrialists.[3] Fürstenberg considered his assembling of this alliance the most noteworthy achievement of his life. The climax of the battle came at a general meeting of the shareholders, at which the anti-treasury forces won a narrow victory and secured it with a further financial manoever. As a consequence of these efforts, the Hibernia firm remained in private hands and the private ownership of capital was defended. In rallying behind this principle, the banks gave expression to their common ideological outlook and revealed the power they could wield when acting in concert.

Rather different problems arise in describing Kreditbanken relations with industry. The basic tool kit with which the banks approached an industrial firm is well known. Short-term credit in one of its several

---

[1] Fürstenberg, p. 401.

[2] Ibid.

[3] Kirdorf was the general director of the Gelsenkirchener mining firm and a very influential figure in mining circles. It has been argued that Furstenberg was acting at Kirdorf's request to prevent the Prussian government from using the Hibernia frim to influence the pricing policies of the Rhenish-Westphalian coal cartel. On this question see: H. Mottek, "Zur Verstaatlichung im Kapitalismus--der Fall Hibernia," Jahrbuch für Wirtschaftsgeschichte, IV (1968), 11 ff.

forms was of primary importance in such relations. Concealed in the intimate details of limits and terms lay the strengths or weaknesses of each of the partners in the eyes of the other. Once a working relationship was established, the way was clear for securities issue. The reputations which made such securities issues possible were jealously guarded assets of the Kreditbanken and a principal attraction drawing industrial firms to them. The size of a securities issue, the terms of its sale, and its success were all determined to a significant extent by the leading bank. Access to the securities markets for larger issues came only through one of the major banks, the support of which usually brought together and thereafter kept together a large syndicate. Under these circumstances it could be risky for a firm to change banks because such changes often gave rise to rumors about the firm's affairs that adversely influenced the prices of the firm's securities. The possibility that such a change would be initiated by a bank added considerable force to that bank's views in its relations with a given firm. So solicitous were industrial firms of their good names in banking circles that even a change in the quota of a bank in a securities consortium was handled with the greatest tact and discretion.

A less well-know tool of the banks in their relations with industry was what is today called "management consulting." When granting short-term credit and establishing a position as the promoter of a firm's securities, a bank would as a matter of course keep well informed about the firm's affairs usually by placing a senior bank official on the firm's board of directors. The nature of such a position might appear routine, but the quality of advice and information provided by bank directors and the depth of understanding of and involvement in firms' affairs were quite remarkable. The purview of an experienced bank director included not only financial questions but those relating to marketing, personnel and often even technology. Such knowledge provided a valuable complement to the banker's financial skills.

With such tools in hand what aims did bankers pursue? Profits were, of course, a main goal of banks. The leading Kreditbanken appear to have been run along lines roughly approximating a modern portfolio approach to risk and anticipated return, although such a judgment can be no more than impressionistic given the state of remaining records. Consistent with such an approach was a desire for stability in the markets supplied by the industrial firms which the banks served. Instability jeopardized not only the interests of such firms but also those of the banks whose credit supported them. This similarity of bank and industrial interests may also be seen in the German penetration of export markets.[1] To the banks such markets were valuable for both the benefits they brought to German industry and for the profits which the banks gained from a growing volume of foreign transactions. It was hoped that as the volume of foreign transactions increased, German financial independence from London would grow as well.

The common aims of the banking community referred to above raise a number of thorny issues. Perhaps the most controversial of these is the question of whether the relations of the major Kreditbanken with industry affected industrial competition. Because the three decades prior to World War I were a period of growing cartelization of German industry,

---

[1]Riesser (English edition), pp. 527-546.

critics of this tendency have sought villians that could be blamed for it. Banks have always been likely candidates, but such a claim needs careful scrutiny. The evidence that is available suggests that banks did not initiate efforts at cartel organization. Rather, they appear to have been the faithful servants of, and often mediators among, the industrial interests they served. There were no grounds in German law or custom to do otherwise.

Admirers of the *Kreditbanken* have suggested a second issue arising from the relations of these banks to industry. Did German industry reap any gains in efficiency that could be attributed to the services of *Kreditbanken*? Bank credit policy may have led to such efficiency gains. Furthermore, the "management consulting" services may have improved the efficiency of the industries receiving them. Archival evidence and secondary accounts both suggest that such effects upon industrial efficiency were plausible. In this case it is not necessary to rely on an impressionistic judgment, since an econometric test of this question is presented in Chapter IV. The proper interpretation of this test depends, however, on an understanding of the capacity of the *Kreditbanken* to produce the effects described above.

There are two additional fields in which issues of bank influence can be raised: the rate of introduction of new technology, and the rate of increase of German industrial exports. Since the record in both of these fields was quite good in the era before World War I, the institutional arrangements in the industries that produced this record ought to get some of the credit for it. Banks were a significant part of those arrangments. Moreover, there is broad agreement, supported by some evidence, that the banks were active promoters of German exports and were inclined to support the introduction of new technology.[1] Whether these efforts benefited the entire industrial economy or merely certain sectors is not known with certainty, nor could anything beyond a vague judgment be given about the extent of any such benefits.

Such general observations provide some understanding of the role of the Kreditbanken in industrial finance. A more finely etched picture may be obtained by examining a part of the record of one bank in one industry. For this purpose, the involvement of the Deutsche Bank in the electrical industry has been chosen. By way of background it should be noted that the history of the German electrical industry has been dominated by two firms: Siemens and Halske, and the Allgemeine Elektricitäts-Gesellschaft.[2] The former firm was founded in the 1850's and owed its success largely to the leadership of Werner von Siemens and his brothers. In 1883 the latter firm was created by Emil Rathenau in close collaboration with Siemens and Halske, to which the A.E.G. remained tied by contracts for some years. These two firms made the major contributions to the development of electric power generation and transmission, electric transportation and various low-and-high voltage applications in Germany. The A.E.G. had ties to the Deutsche Bank that went back to the firm's founding. The bank's relations to Siemens and Halske were especially close because Georg Siemens, cousin and former employee of Werner von Siemens, was a

---

[1]Fritz Seidenzahl, 100 Jahre Deutsche Bank, 1870-1970 (Frankfurt am Main: Johannes Weisbecker, 1970), p. 186 ff.

[2]For a brief account of the structure of the German electrical industry in this era see: F. Fasolt, Die sieben grössten Elektrizitätsgesellschaften, ihre Entwicklung und Unternehmertätigkeit (Dresden: Böhmert, 1904).

leading figure of the Deutsche Bank from its inception. Having been so closely associated with both firms gave the Deutsche Bank a pivotal position in the electrical industry.

These relations will first be used to show the degree to which banks became involved in the affairs of the firms they served. Securities issue is a field in which such involvement could easily be seen. Of interest in this context is an 1898 Siemens and Halske bond issue which the Deutsche Bank managed. The critical question in such securities issues were the composition of the issuing consortium and the quotas of the various members. The correspondence between the bank and Siemens and Halske reveals the careful judgments upon which agreement had to be reached before the bond issue could take place.

Arthur von Gwinner, a director of the Deutsche Bank, first presented the bank's plan for the issue to Herr Bödiker of the Siemens and Halske Vorstand (top management). Gwinner noted that the Disconto-Gesellschaft had accepted a full share in the issue at which "in the interests of Siemens and Halske" he took great pleasure. In deference to the wishes of the Disconto-Gesellschaft he intended to give a half share to the Norddeutsche Bank of Hamburg, which he described as "one of the most important provincial German banks."[1] A second such request of the Disconto-Gesellschaft was refused because the provincial bank in question was not considered sufficiently prominent. The strength and prestige of the various banks mentioned was the focus of these remarks. Additional considerations came into play in remarks concerning the

[1] Letter from A. Gwinner to Dr. Bodiker, 31 March 1898.

Darmstädter Bank. Gwinner pointed out that since other banks of the "union group," the banks that belonged to the consortium that issued the securities of the Union Electric Company, had been included, it would have been an insult not to include the Darmstädter. With the characteristic subtlety of the banker, he called attention to the "considerable influence of this bank with the Berlin municipal government." Prudence required that good relations be maintained with these banks whose good will could be helpful to Siemens and Halske.

Where such benefit could not be expected, a different response was called for. Gwinner proposed that the banking firm of Delbrück, Leo and Company, which received a full share in the previous Siemens and Halske consortium (of 1893) be limited to three-quarters of a share in the new consortium. He did so because Delbrück, Leo and Company had to a great extent associated itself with a competing group. Bödiker's reply indicates that only on this point did he disagree on the ground that "Herr Delbrück, who has had business ties with our house for many years, would very gladly show himself to be friendly to our house [if given a full share]."[1] Gwinner's tart reply clarified the question. "I do not doubt the willingness of D. L. & Co. [Delbrück, Leo and Company] to show themselves friendly to Siemens and Halske, but their ability," he wrote, "since they are contractually bound to deal exclusively with A.E.G. in the electrical field."[2] The original distribution proposed by the Deutsche Bank was accepted and the bonds were issued as

---

[1]Letter from Bödiker to Gwinner, 1 April 1898.

[2]Letter from Gwinner to Bodiker, 2 April 1898.

planned. In June, 1898, Gwinner was able to report that the Siemens and Halske bonds had been placed satisfactorily. Only one minor difficulty was reported when Delbrück, Leo and Company offered the bonds under the daily closing price by printed circular (!), an action that could "discredit them in the eyes of the public." The Deutsche Bank took steps to end this disruptive practice immediately.

The extent to which the Deutsche Bank was entrusted with the protection of the financial interests of Siemens and Halske is well illustrated in this case. A tactful but firm diplomacy was needed to prevent the firm from incurring the disfavor of strong banks or from being harmed by the questionable practices of weak ones. This protective function rested mainly on the financial strength and superior sources of information of the Deutsche Bank, which enabled the bank to manage such securities issues with relative ease. These characteristics of the bank enabled it to be helpful to Siemens and Halske in other fields as well. Since a firm's fate depended on many factors besides access to the capital market, such assistance from the Deutsche Bank was welcome, especially in such intricate matters as mergers.

Immediately after the turn of the century, the German electrical industry entered a period of severe crisis. Of the seven firms, or more accurately, groups of firms in the industry, one collapsed and the remainder began to consider mergers.[1] The merger negotiations were extremely complex, rather like dynastic marriage politics with the various

---

[1]These groups were the Siemens and Halske group, the A.E.G. group, the Schuckert group, the Union (or Loewe) group, the Helios group, the Lahmeyer group and the Kummer group. Of these, the first four were the major forces in the industry.

banking groups having taken roles of family members whose endorsement was needed to make a match. An item from the minutes of the February 11, 1902, meeting of the Board of Directors of Siemens and Halske shows that a merger between the A.E.G. and Schuckert groups were under consideration, leaving open the possibility that Siemens and Halske would later join in. The final realignment of the electrical industry was along entirely different lines, and the reasons may be traced in several cryptic notes pencilled in at the bottom of the Deutsche Bank's copy of these minutes, which read:

> for us a combination with the A.E.G. would be much easier that one with the Union with whose bankers close cooperation has always proved impossible.
>
> Steinthal
>
> but Rath[enau] thinks so much more of himself than of all the others including S & H [Siemens and Halske] that an understanding would hardly be possible, rather with Loewe.
>
> M[anciewicz]
>
> I see the value of an understanding with Loewe only from the negative side.
>
> Gw[inner][1]

Each of these men was a top-level officer of the Deutsche Bank. It is evident from their comments that a consensus could not be obtained in favor of either of the alliances mentioned.

There is no evidence that these bankers dictated or attempted to dictate a merger policy to the industry. One did not dictate to either the Siemens family or Emil Rathenau in any case. On the other

---

[1] Siemens and Halske, Minutes of the 11 February 1902 Board of Directors.

hand, the realignment of the industry that followed in 1903, the merger of the A.E.G. and Union groups and the partial merger of Siemens and Schuckert is the only outcome which the notes quoted above left open. What this fact suggests is that the three authors of those notes had a keen understanding of the individuals and institutions concerned and more than a modicum of influence with the conservative Siemens family. The available correspondence does not allow a complete reconstruction of the merger negotiations. All that can be shown is that Siemens and Halske remained in close contact with the Deutsche Bank during this period and that the bank enthusiastically supported the arrangements linking Siemens and Halske to Schuckert. The Deutsche Bank showed its support by rounding up 2,500,000 marks worth of Schuckert shares, the votes of which were used to approve the Siemens-Schuckert plan.[1] A broad interpretation of the evidence leads to the conclusion that the bank played a significant but discreet role in the crucial merger decisions of these years.

There were also numerous examples of the involvement of the Deutsche Bank in affairs of Siemens and Halske whose bearing on financial matters were less obvious. When in 1903 labor agitation began at Siemens and Halske, its management formulated a plan to deal with it. Werner von Siemens sent the plan to Ludwig Roland-Lucke, one of the Deutsche Bank's directors on the Siemens and Halske board, for careful review.[1] The plan was not put into effect before Siemens obtained the bank's advice. The firm's sales efforts were also not spared the critical judgment of its

---

[1]Letter from Werner von Siemens to Roland-Lucke, 24 August 1903.

bankers. Since the bank did what it could to help firms it served to win foreign contracts, bank directors could become quite irritated when firms did not compete as aggressively as it was thought they should. Such a situation developed in 1906 when the Rand Central Electric Works was granting contracts for which the A.E.G. and Siemens and Halske were competing. The Deutsche Bank, which had a major role in South African finance, had been making strenuous efforts on behalf of Siemens and Halske, so that the apparently sluggish sales campaign of Siemens was particularly annoying. Max Steinthal, who had followed the matter closely, complained that "the Siemens concern had limited itself to answering [technical] questions and did not show a shred of initiative in undermining the technical claims of the competition."[1] The Deutsche Bank itself had to "inspire" a vigorous defense of the interests of Siemens and Halske in this case.

What this and previous cases show is a quite distinct pattern of bank involvement in the affairs of Siemens and Halske. Such involvement ranged from securities issues and mergers to the firm's labor policy and sales efforts. Yet the Deutsche Bank was careful to maintain a proper respect for the independence of Siemens and Halske, and the firm's independence did not suffer because of its ties to the bank. Nonetheless, situations did arise in which the bank made use of its rather potent influence in a very direct manner. Although in such cases the bank always acted in the best interests of the firm, the bank's stance could limit--sometimes severely--the freedom of action of Siemens and Halske.

---

[1]Letter from Roland-Lucke to Berliner, 15 December 1906.

To gauge the strength of bank influence, several relevant examples of its use will be explored.

During the latter years of Georg Siemens' career at the Deutsche Bank his defense of the corporate interests of Siemens and Halske brought him into frequent and sometimes serious conflict with the family-oriented approach of the Siemens brothers.[1] Such conflict between the bank and the firm continued after Georg Siemens' death in 1901. One well-documented instance concerned the tenure of Dr. Berliner, the director of Siemens-Schuckert Electric Works. Dr. Berliner wanted his authority as chief operating officer of the firm better delineated and protected from the interference of Wilhelm von Siemens, the chairman of the board of directors. A Deutsche Bank director on the board of Siemens and Halske, Roland-Lücke, supported Dr. Berliner, and both men threatened to resign if the matter were not resolved in Dr. Berliner's favor.[2] Siemens took Roland-Lücke's threat seriously because such a resignation would have been sure to stimulate undesirable speculation in the financial press. So great was public concern with the state of the bank's relation with the firm that determined efforts were made by Siemens to avoid an open sign of disagreement.

Siemens responded to the threat with an earnest letter presenting his side of the dispute to Roland-Lücke. Explaining Berliner's claim, Siemens wrote:

> B's [Berliner's] theory is basically that a unified leadership of the firm is impossible as a consequence of the influence that I exercise

---

[1] For a good treatment, see: Seidenzahl, p. 134 ff.

[2] Dr. Berliner wanted to be appointed Generaldirector of the firm.

> on the operations of the management. In spite of my explanation to the contrary, you have become convinced during a conversation with B. that due to my influence the head of management cannot have the quick, appropriate control that a proper initiative requires.[1]

This argument was dismissed by Siemens who attributed the problem to a personality clash. Roland-Lücke's tactful reply argued that Siemens could remain a strong board chairman

> without making impossible unified, capable, and responsive leadership by the management [Vorstand] and a general director. Naturally such a management would be obliged to conduct the firm's affairs with the constant agreement of the chairman of the board in more important matters. In contrast to the present situation only one distinction need be introduced. Communications or wishes which the chairman makes known to one or another member of the management as an expression of close collaboration should immediately and voluntarily be made known to the focal point of the management, the general director. In this way unified operations will be insured . . . [2]

There is no mistaking the issue which this disagreement raised. Both the internal structure and the leadership of Siemens-Schuckert Works were at stake. Roland-Lücke most likely saw the dispute as a conflict between the firm's interests and the interests of the Siemens family. While this conflict was an on-going one, it appears that Roland-Lücke and Berliner won this round, for both men kept their positions. The incident illustrates that even moderate but subtly applied pressure from the Deutsche Bank could have a serious impact on Siemens and Halske.

---

[1] Letter from Werner von Siemens to Roland-Lücke, 1 December 1906.

[2] Letter from Roland-Lücke to Werner von Siemens, 3 December 1906.

There were circumstances under which such pressure could become severe. It is a commonplace of banking that the liquidity position of current-account borrowers bears close watching. The danger of a liquidity crisis is that the funds to repay short-term bank loans may be absent when such loans come due. Siemens and Halske experienced such a crisis early in 1901 and the response of the Deutsche Bank was very firm. An account of the crisis was given in a 1903 letter of Werner von Siemens that dealt with his firm's liquidity. Siemens wrote:

> . . . I was urgently requested to come to the Deutsche Bank, and I believe that the entire <u>Direktion</u> of the Deutsche Bank was gathered there. My deceased cousin [Georg von Siemens] told me that our company did not have enough money and asked how it should be raised. Herr Gwinner judged that we needed 5 or 6 million. It was not possible to issue shares or bonds and under no circumstances could we count on the Deutsche Bank to advance us the money. I answered for a comfortable and financially strong position there were indeed several million lacking. But I believed that at the present time we would get by and certainly not be obliged at least for the time being to approach the banks. My comments were received with great skepticism and my family was required to obligate itself for two years to lend the firm its last dividend of ten per cent.[1]

What is surprising here is not the attitude of the Deutsche Bank, but rather than of Werner von Siemens. It is not clear why Werner von Siemens thought that the Deutsche Bank would allow his firm's liquidity position to worsen and would then accept the resulting risk itself. Any such illusions on his part were quickly dispelled when the bank held his firm to the most rigid rules of good financial practice. The bank's

---

[1]Letter from Werner von Siemens to Roland-Lücke, 15 August 1902.

conduct in this liquidity crisis shows that in the field of finance, in which the bank's responsibility to exert some influence over the affairs of Siemens and Halske was clearest, the bank acted with vigor.

While bank influence most commonly made itself felt in the financial and managerial policies of Siemens and Halske, this influence could be detected in other fields as well. Moreover, the bank's influence was not always used in a restrictive way. When in the bank's view Siemens and Halske was treated unfairly by purchasers of the firm's products, the bank might well find a way to intervene in order to defend Siemens' interests. Just such a situation developed during the winter of 1913-1914. An informal agreement had apparently been worked out according to which Siemens and Halske and the A.E.G. were to share evenly the contracts being granted by the Constantinople Tramways Company. To the former firm's surprise, the agents of the latter won all of the electric motor contracts. The manoever was apparently based on a false allegation of technical problems in Siemens' motors. Siemens and Halske was incensed at the loss of the contracts, not only because of their monetary value, but also because of the implied challenge to the firm's technical competence. Lacking any other recourse Simens and Halske appealed to Elkan Heinemann, the representative of the Deutsche Bank on the Siemens board at that time.

In this case the Deutsche Bank had especially good channels through which to make its influence felt. The Constantinople project was being financed by the Société Financière de Transportes et d'Entreprises Industrielles of Brussels, a leading figure of which, D. Heinemann, had worked in close collaboration with the Deutsche Bank for many years in the Deutsche Überseeische Elektricitats-Gesellschaft. E. Heinemann sent a telegram to D. Heineman protesting the exclusion of Siemens from the motor contracts and followed up with a strongly worded letter supporting Siemens' position and defending its technical competence. E. Heinemann pointed out that:

> the Siemens-Schuckert Works could not possibly allow itself to be denied contracts for motors . . . Also considering the matter from the standpoint of the Deutsche Bank, I must make the friendly request that you see to it that the Siemens-Schuckert Works is not unfairly treated.[1]

In spite of these efforts, the response from Brussels included only temporizing and excuses.

The Deutsche Bank could not be put off with such temporizing. E. Heinemann sent to Brussels an even more pointedly worded letter repeating Siemens' case and providing technical information and an engineer's report to support it. A technical report from Constantinople confirmed the adequacy of the Siemens motors, but the results of these tests were questioned and a second series of tests were conducted with the same result. On March 6, D. Heineman informed the Deutsche Bank that the motor contracts were to be divided equally between the A.E.G. and Siemens and Halske. It is doubtful that technical factors alone prompted this decision. Although the record offers no certainly on this point, there is reason to suspect that the Deutsche Bank gave the Société Financière a disturbing example of the future treatment its interests could receive,

---

[1]Letter from E. Heinemann to D. Heineman in Brussels, 4 February 1914.

if the Société Financière did not respect Siemens' interests in this affair. In his letter of thanks to Brussels, E. Heinemann wrote:

> I want to thank you for your friendly efforts in this matter.
>
> I would also like to take this opportunity to mention that the Banco Aleman Transatlantico in Barcelona has decided after further consideration that it will agree after all to an extension of its 100,000 peso loan to the streetcar company. This is being done because the company has again explained that it would find such an extension extremely valuable in view of negotiations to be conducted with the gentelemen concerned.[1]

What this letter suggests is that the Deutsche Bank used its influence with a bank in Barcelona to have a sizable, and possibly badly needed, credit withdrawn from a company in which the Société Financière had an interest. After the Société Financière had arranged the Turkish motor contracts in a way that the Deutsche Bank found satisfactory, the credit was reinstated. One wonders how Siemens and Halske would have fared in such situations had it not been possible to call upon the influence of the Deutsche Bank to defend Siemens' interests.

Although the Deutsche Bank could make its influence felt through discreet gestures like the one described above, the power of the bank should not be overestimated. The use of bank influence was subject to severe limitations, some obvious, others less so. Obvious limitations included potential or actual government regulation and keen competition among bankers.[2] The less obvious limitations are best explained by

---

[1] Letter from E. Heinemann to D. Heineman in Brussels, 9 March 1914.

[2] The Bank Enquete of 1908 is evidence of parliamentary concern for possible abuses in banking.

example, and the first such example concerns a situation rather like the dispute about electric motor contracts. The Deutsche Bank had had close relations with the Mannesmann Works, a major German metallurgical concern, ever since the firm's founding. Because of this connection, Dr. Berliner (or Siemens-Schuckert) thought that Siemens had the favored position to obtain Mannesmann's electrical contracts. When in the spring of 1905 a major turbine contract went to the A.E.G., Berliner became very irritated and expressed his irritation in several very candid letters to Roland-Lücke.

The main issue that Berliner raised in this correspondence was the extent to which the Deutsche Bank was obligated to direct contracts for electrical equipment to Siemens and Halske. Berliner's interpretation of this obligation went very far indeed, as his remarks showed:

> I don't want to close this letter without making you aware of the fact that we are still bound to the Deutsche Bank by a contractual relationship. And the Deutsche Bank has the duty to help us obtain business in every way and not, as in the preceding case, to allow the competition to win business that a stroke of the pen would have given to us.[1]

A second letter continued in the same vein, noting that "we regret terribly that the Mannesmann Works shows so little concern for the relations that exist between you and us . . ."[2] For the bank such an understanding of these relations went a good deal too far. Such a carte blanche was quite out of the question. The Deutsche Bank knew that its

---

[1] Letter from Berliner to Roland-Lücke, 24 May 1905.

[2] Letter from Berliner to Klönne, 24 May 1905.

officers and not those of Siemens and Halske were the proper judges of what support could have been and ought to have been given that firm, and the bank reacted accordingly.

The banks' response emphasized the limits of its influence. After investigating the granting of the contract, Roland-Lücke reported that Mannesmann's decision was based on technical factors but that he assumed that a poor sales effort by Siemens and Halske was also to blame. He added that "on the side of the Deutsche Bank everything has been done which can be done in such cases; coercion (Diktieren) of the sort you take for granted is not possible."[1] Concerning the "contractual relationship" between bank and firm, Roland-Lücke noted that Berliner's interpretation of that relationship was not acceptable and that he and his colleagues were considering the termination of this contractual relationship because they could not approve Berliner's view. Berliner backed down immediately replying that his remarks had not been interpreted as he had intended. Claiming that he understood the Deutsche Bank could not guarantee Siemens the electrical contracts of every firm with which the bank was friendly, Berliner maintained that he had merely wanted help in winning technically challenging contracts.[2] Berliner's effort was not wasted, since Siemens did obtain some less important Mannesmann contracts. The Deutsche Bank used the incident to demonstrate that there were definite limits beyond which it would not go in assisting friendly firms and that the bank determined where those limits lay.

Nowhere were the limitations of the influence of the Deutsche Bank exposed more clearly than in some of the American projects in which

---

[1] Letter from Roland-Lücke to Berliner, 27 May 1905.

[2] Letter from Berliner to Roland-Lücke, 27 May 1905.

the bank became involved. The participation of the Deutsche Bank in the financing of the Northern Pacific Railroad cost the bank's officers years of effort and vexation.[1] An American project in the electrical industry, in which the Deutsche Bank joined Siemens and Halske and the A.E.G., was an equally ill-fated venture from the German point of view. In 1893 some loose ends of this affair remained to be settled and Georg Siemens travelled to American for this purpose. One of these loose ends was the Deutsche Bank's stake in the Cincinnati Light Company, which was floundering. Georg Siemens was attempting to shore it up and contacted Rathenau in hopes of getting his help and advice. Rathenau, who had recently inspected American electrical installations, advised him that he "had never before seen such wretchedly patched together machinery"as that which General Edison Electric Company had supplied to Cincinnati.[2] In Rathenau's judgment the machinery was not likely to last more than a year, if that long. Rathenau's advice was easier to obtain than his help. Neither the A.E.G. nor Siemens and Halske gave the Deutsche Bank any assistance in this case. This relatively minor incident shows that the extent to which a bank could call upon its industrial collaborators for assistance could be extremely limited.

The most fundamental problem that the bank faced in the course of its involvement with the German electrical industry was in fact keeping the peace.[3] As a result of patent considerations and financial

---

[1]See: Seidenzahl, p. 83 ff.

[2]Letter from Steinthal to Georg Siemens in Chicago, 27 October 1893.

[3]For a good discussion of Georg Siemens' career and some interesting excerpts from his letters, see: Karl Helferich, Georg von Siemens (Berlin: Verlag von Julius Springer, 1923).

problems, the A.E.G., or rather its predecessor the Deutsche Edison Gesellschaft, began its existence as a stepchild of Siemens and Halske.[1] The two firms were bound together by a ten year contract which resolved patent conflicts, gave the A.E.G. precedence in the building of central power stations and obligated the A.E.G. to purchase most of its heavy equipment (e.g., dynamos and cable) from Siemens and Halske. Although drastically revised in 1887, this contract gave rise to intense friction and disagreement between the parties. Such tension put Georg Siemens in a very difficult position. The Deutsche Bank was the leader of the syndicate for the issue of A.E.G. securities and Georg Siemens was first a prominent member and then (from 1889 until 1896) the chairman of the A.E.G. board of directors. At the same time Georg Siemens had close personal, family and professional ties to Siemens and Halske. What was his proper role?

In a letter to Georg Siemens written at the time that the troublesome contract between the two firms was finally being terminated, Emil Rathenau described Siemens as an "honest broker" ("*ehrlicher Makler*").[2] Rathenau was surely among those best placed to make such a judgment, and Siemens' correspondence with others fully supports Rathenau's view. How faithfully Georg Siemens played this role is illustrated by an 1888 letter from Siemens to Henry Villard, the American financier in whom Siemens often confided:

---

[1] Rathenau's firm was orginally organized in 1883 as the Deutsche Edison Gesellschaft. In 1887 the firm was reorganized and assumed the name "Allgemeine Electricitats Gesellschaft."

[2] Letter from Rathenau to Georg Siemens, 19 May 1894.

> The conflict between Siemens and Halske and the General Electric Company [A.E.G.] becomes sharper and sharper and cooperation between the two more and more problematical. To my regret the fault appears to be to a great degree on the side of Siemens and Halske.[1]

Family ties did not obscure Siemens' view of his relatives' faults or confuse his judgment of the merits and weaknesses of their case. He did his discreet best to make each side consider the position of the other. Yet the seemingly endless quarreling that he witnessed must have tried his patience. His correspondence often betrays more than a hint of frustration:

> It is a pity that face to face dealings are so difficult between you two [Rathenau and Werner von Siemens]. I believe that a conversation could be quite useful. I lack any knowledge of technical matters and the "pre-history," so that I am not able to distinguish the essential from the non-essential. I am even afraid that I am not useful enough as a referee and broker between the parties.[2]

Given the obstacles he faced, Georg Siemens was not only useful, he was astonishingly successful in maintaining a degree of peace that allowed the German electrical industry to prosper.

The record of Georg Siemens' dealing with Rathenau offers ironic testimony to this success. During the late 1880's when the A.E.G. was gravely threatened by the actions of Siemens and Halske, George Siemens fought tirelessly to keep Rathenau's firm afloat. The letters of Georg Siemens to his cousin Werner contain frequent references to a possible

---

[1] Letter from Georg Siemens to Henry Villard in Eisenach, 11 June 1888.

[2] Letter from Georg Siemens to Werner von Siemens, 12 June 1888.

failure of the A.E.G. Such a failure, Georg Siemens argued, would do Siemens and Halske no good. Rather, "a failure of the company [A.E.G.] will be blamed finally on you [Werner von Siemens], Delbrück and me . . . the publicity will of course first focus on you . . . "[1] These telling arguments had the intended effect, and the compromise fashioned almost single-handedly by Georg Siemens was accepted by all parties. In the absence of such a compromise it is quite possible that the A.E.G. would have failed.

Instead of a failure, Rathenau had a brilliant and remarkable success. By the latter part of the 1890's, Georg Siemens' correspondence concerning Rathenau took on a decidedly different tone:

> R's [Rathenau's] ambition is to gather around himself the greatest possible number of bankers and to withdraw them from the competition. Therefore he requires from bankers that they bind themselves to him irrevocably for six years.[2]

From the point of view of the Deutsche Bank, Rathenau's plan to form a securities consortium was entirely unacceptable. With a display of his familiar diplomatic skill, Georg Siemens convinced Rathenau to eliminate the objectionable exclusivity provision from Rathenau's proposal. A mere decade earlier Siemens had been fighting to keep Rathenau's firm alive; now Siemens was manoevering to prevent Rathenau from obtaining unreasonable concessions from the Deutsche Bank.

---

[1] Letter from Georg Siemens to Werner von Siemens, 18 May 1888.

[2] Letter from Georg Siemens to Abegg in Zurich, 26 December 1896.

When it came to direct clashes of such giants as Werner von Siemens and Emil Rathenau, the true limitations on the influence of the Deutsche Bank emerged most clearly. Straining his every resource, a banker as gifted as Georg Siemens was barely able to keep the peace. His was the role of mediator. Such stability as existed in the electrical industry in its critical early years was due in no small measure to his efforts. The skill and fairness of these efforts as mediator certainly belie any charge of deliberate abuse of power. In view of the limitations he faced, his accomplishment is as surprising as it is impressive.

With the help of some familiarity with the experience of the Kreditbanken in industrial finance in the period before World War I, Riesser's interpretation can be reconsidered. If the development of the electrical industry is at all representative of that of German industry as a whole, then Riesser provides an accurate description of the place of the Kreditbanken. Where that description leads is not entirely clear. In great detail Riesser explains the interdependence of banks and industry, the chief consequence of which is a high degree of organization (i.e., by merger, cartel, etc.) among each. There are also suggestions about the consequences of a less organized, "concentrated" banking system:

> Unquestionably the business policy of a great bank . . . can and will be carried out more in accordance with a uniform program, which takes into account the general economic interests including those of the Government. Such a policy can be pursued by it much more readily than by a moderate-size or small bank or by a large number of small scattered banks, which are compelled to shape their policy merely with a view of dividends.[1]

---

[1] Riesser (English edition), p. 754.

Riesser's evidence of such a "policy" on the part of the Kreditbanken includes encouragement of German exports and foreign investment and cooperation in developjng social overhead capital and shipping. The maintenance of more stable economic conditions, or at least more stable credit markets, is also claimed to be a part of this "policy." Since Riesser de-emphasizes the danger of monopoly in banking, the issue of the possibility of greater competition under a different banking system does not arise. Riesser's comparative argument is of great historical interest but is not sufficient to resolve the counter-factual question it raises.[1] The interesting aspect of this argument is its suggestion that the banks did not carry out a strictly profit-maximizing policy. In any case, evidence from both Riesser and the archives of the Deutsche Bank shows that the banks had the capacity to carry out such a policy of national scope, and the record also strongly suggests that they did so.

Taking off from this "policy" question, the point at which Riesser's interpretation stops, one faces one very formidable question. Assuming that the Kreditbanken pursued such a "policy," whose policy was it?

---

[1] Because the primary focus of this discussion is bank policy toward industry, factors making possible industrial independence from banks are not emphasized. Chief among these factors was the undistributed profits of industrial firms which allowed substantial self-financing and the accumulation of large reserves. For a very helpful treatment of this matter see: Walther Hoffmann, "Die unverteilten Gewinne der Kapitalgesellschaften in Deutschland, 1871-1957," Zeitschrift für die Gesamte Staatswissenschaft, CXV (1959), 271-291.

Did they act on their own behalf? Were the banks the passive instruments of the industrialists who used the banks' services? Or was the government dictating policy to banks and industry alike? The available archival evidence offers no reliable answer to this question. In any case, the salient fact remains that any "policymaker" would have found the *Kreditbanken* powerful collaborators in pursuing economic goals. At the very least the passive acceptance of the banks would have been needed to make any policy viable. The Hibernia Mines did, after all, remain in private hands.

When the goals of the *Kreditbanken* and those influencing them are not precisely known, judging the performance of the banks is quite difficult. Such a judgment cannot be made without a standard, and there are not many suitable standards to try. The views of contemporaries are helpful but cannot be conclusive. There is no way to correct for the biases to which contemporaries are often susceptible. Well-chosen historical comparisons can yield useful insights. The problem with such an approach is that there are no theoretical tools for making such comparisons among national economies so that the performance of a banking system cannot be separated from many other factors whose influence ought to be excluded. A last possible approach is to specify a goal of bank policy which is reasonable from a theoretical point of view and which does not conflict with available evidence. Under certain circumstances an econometric test can be carried out that measures the success of the banking system with respect to the goal specified. In the following chapter, this approach is used to reach a judgment of the performance of the *Kreditbanken* in the period 1883 to 1913.

CHAPTER IV

AN ECONOMETRIC TEST OF THE ROLE OF THE KREDITBANKEN: 1883-1913

The era from unification to World War I was one of continuing industrialization in Germany. Regardless of the preferences or ideological views of other segments of German society, the business community supported industrial development with enthusiasm. The enthusiasm of no other group surpassed that of the leading figures of the *Kreditbanken*. Assuming that their outlook or "policy" reflected both their own aims and those of the business community in general, what kind of policy "ought" the banks to have followed? On the basis of theoretical considerations and the prominent features of the historical record, one would expect that the banks allocated their credit, and in a broader sense, their attention, to those fields where the return was highest. Such a policy would have contributed to the attainment of maximum levels of output. In an economic setting like that of Imperial Germany in which the development of capital intensive industries predominated, such efficient credit allocation would have resulted in a rapid increase in the level of output. Just such an increase is an easily recognizable feature of the record of these years. On these bases, a policy of efficient credit allocation will be assumed on the part of the *Kreditbanken*.

This assumption is very much in keeping with both long-standing and recent scholarly views of the German banking system in that era. A recent, thought-provoking treatment is Die Beeinflussung des Wirtschaftswachtums in Deutschland von 1883 bis 1913 durch das Bankensystem of Ekkehard Eistert. Eistert's most significant conclusion is that ". . . the behavior of the banks either made easier or actually made possible the growth of [German] national income . . ."[1] In this context, "behavior" refers to the granting of what the author considers credit, (i.e., credit for expenditures that contribute to national income, excluding what he considers speculative credit). Eistert's study consists of theoretical observations about the nature of bank credit and a substantial amount of empirical work. Its empirical content includes a reliable data set for different categories of bank credit and some rather straight-forward statistical correlation. Although Eistert's approach is useful, it seems clear that econometric techniques can be employed to probe more deeply into the role of banks in the growth of German national income in this era.

Structuring a suitable econometric test requires the aid and the perspective offered by a general theory of industrialization. Alexander Gerschenkron's essays, "Economic Backwardness in Historical Perspective" and "Prerequisites of Modern Industrialization," are most suitable for this purpose.[2] In Gerschenkron's view, "backward" countries which experience successful industrializations do so by making institutional "substitutions" which enable them to compensate for or even turn to their

---

[1]Eistert, p. 140.

[2]Gerschenkron, Economic Backwardness in Historical Perspective Cambridge: Harvard University Press, 1962).

advantage their initial deficiences of productive factors. According to Gerschenkron, the institution which compensated for such deficiencies in Germany was the Kreditbank. This interpretation places special emphasis on the growth-inducing character of these banks, but is also open to the possibility that an industrilization led by such institutions might entail costs. In fact, Gerschenkron explicitly invites help in assessing these costs in commenting: "it would be a fruitful undertaking in research to explore and perhaps to measure and compare the difficulties, the strains and the cost which were involved in the various processes of substitution . . ."[1] Making use of the data that Eistert gathered for the period 1883 to 1913, an econometric model has been constructed that attempts such a "fruitful undertaking." This model tests whether the manner in which the Kreditbanken allocated current-account credit contributed to the growth of German non-agricultural output.

The Role of Current-Account Credit

To provide suitable account services to their growing industrial clientele, the Kreditbanken developed a modernized version of an ancient banking practice, the current-account. The current-account is rather like a combined demand-deposit account and line of credit.[2] Interest was paid on credit balances at a rate of one per cent under the Reichsbank discount rate and charged on debit balances at one per cent over that rate plus minor fees. Deposits and withdrawals could be made as

---

[1] Ibid., p. 51.

[2] Siegfried Buff, Das Kontokorrentgeschäft im deutschen Bankgewerbe (Berlin: Cotta'sche Buchhandlung, 1904), p. 47.

the account holder chose provided he did not exceed his line of credit, and settlements were made quarterly. Security required for such account, if any, was usually a mortgage on real property or bonds or shares. Because of their extraordinary flexibility, current-accounts became the predominant form of account service used by German industry.

Not all current-accounts in the Kreditbanken were held by industrial firms, but they held a large part of these accounts so that they received most of the credit extended through them.[1] Since commercial credit was arranged primarily through bills of exchange, such credit does not pose a problem for data on current-accounts. Eistert reports that "current-account credit is chiefly used to provide fixed or working capital to industry. The evidence that current-account credit is used in this way may be found in the annual reports of the banks."[2] Adding to the usefulness of current-account credit as an indicator of the extent of industrial financing by banks is its growth as opposed to that of domestic bill credit. Until 1895 current-account credit grew at a rate only moderately faster than that of domestic bill credit. After that year, the growth of current-account credit accelerated dramatically leaving domestic bill credit far behind. This pattern reflects the deepening of relations between banks and industry caused by the great boom that began in that year. In 1883 domestic bills of exchange made up 42% of total credit extended by all Kreditbanken and current-accounts 50.8%; by 1913 these shares were 20% and 72.8% respectively.[3] This shift indicates the extent

---

[1] Eistert, pp. 89-91. Note that data used in this paper have been corrected to exclude current-account credit extended for other than industrial purposes.

[2] Ibid., p. 91.

[3] Ibid., p. 149.

to which Kreditbanken transferred their attention from commerce to industry over the period as a whole.

To the banks the current-account form offered many advantages, not the least of which was that a large part of bank earnings came from such accounts. Riesser's description of these advantages is so revealing that it is worth reproducing in full:

> Through the current-account the bank serves in the first place in the capacity of "maid of all work" in the business household of its customers, performing a thousand and one services each for a small consideration. This menial position, as a rule, is, however, only a temporary stepping stone in its progress to a position of influence, at times even of dominance, and one offering great advantages of the most diverse kinds.
>
> For this reason the current account more than any other branch of business represents the field in which the various banks fight their competitive battles, particularly the battle for industrial clientele. Once regular relations are established through the current account, a direct road is opened to power and profit for the bank. This road leads past the various forms of loans, which of themselves, especially the right to close the account, give a certain amount of influence to the bank. It leads further to increased power and profit through reorganizations, promotions, floatations of securities, consolidations and permanent ownership, or representation on the supervisory board or both. Through these transactions it leads to the conquest of entire branches of industrial activity, to close affiliation with commanding industrial concerns, cartels, and syndicates, and marks the beginning of the supremacy of groups of banks.[1]

As these observations make abundantly clear, the current-account was the basic nexus between bank and industrial firm.[2] It is important to attempt

---

[1] Riesser (English edition), pp. 259-260.

[2] Also see Jeidels, pp. 121-127.

to disaggregate the effects of this nexus if we are to assess the impact of the German banks on German growth in this period.

The total effect of the German banks on growth can be thought of as comprising a substitution effect, an institutional effect and a credit effect. While the model that is developed in succeeding paragraphs attempts to distinguish these effects, each effect must first be defined. The use of current-account financing was a method by which banks could extend long-term credit to particular industries at short-term rates. The chief consequence to the economy of the banks' use of such accounts was that various heavy industries obtained financing at rates below the free market, long-term rate of interest while other industries paid a correspondingly higher rate of interest. What is implied is that capital was not allocated strictly in accordance with its marginal product in the different sectors. Such a policy brings about a substitution effect which represents an implied inefficiency in the economy system caused by the banking system. Given the institutional intricacies of mixed banking, the Kreditbanken themselves suffered no net loss from this policy and so remained good profit maximizers. Any loss to the banks implied by their credit policy was more than counterbalanced by lowered costs of information about the firms they served and enhanced opportunities for profitable securities issue and sale.[1] Under such circumstances a cost of the banks' credit policy to the entire non-agricultural economy could have resulted which the banks may never have perceived. If the banking system actually contributed to growth, then this cost must have been offset by other effects.

[1]For an explanation of the meaning of current-accounts from the banks' side, see Buff, pp. 57-67.

Such possible effects include an institutional effect and a credit effect. The credit effect arises from the fact that in general an economy will grow if there is more credit available providing that such credit does not stimulate an unstable inflation causing widespread disruption to the economy. Any test of the effect of the special institutions of the German banking system must correct for the credit effect, since this effect is characteristic of all banking systems. What must be tested is whether there is something to be gained from the special German institutional arrangements. If there is such a gain, it may be called the institutional effect. While it is clear that the substitution effect will lower potential output and the credit effect will raise potential output, it is unclear whether the institutional effect will raise or lower output. On the one hand a case could be made that the banks assisted certain industries significantly insofar as the banks were able to improve relations between various firms in an industry and this function resulted in a net gain to the industry. On the other hand, a case could be made there were serious diseconomies in the institutional arrangement that gave the banks positions on the boards of the various firms in an industry.

Our task is to filter out the credit effect and measure the credit-constant total effect which consists of the institutional effect, the sign of which is unknown, and the substitution effect which has a negative sign. Our model will determine exactly the sign of the credit-constant total effect. This sign will in some cases give a sure indication of the sign of the institutional effect. For example, if the credit-constant total effect is positive, then the institutional effect must be positive, since the latter must have outweighed the substitution effect which is known to be negative. On the other hand, if the credit-constant total effect is negative, signifying that on balance the growth of current-account financing caused a reduction in the potential output of the German economy, then it cannot be determined directly whether the institutional effect is positive or negative.[1]

The preceding sections suggest that although the current-account is the mechanism by which the banks established their close connections with certain industries, the total amount of current-account credit is not a sufficient measure to determined the effect of the German banks upon growth. Difficulties would arise because such a measure confuses the credit effect with the substitution and institutional effects. What is needed is a measure of the extent of involvement of the banking system with industry that is adjusted for the total credit extended by the banking system. This measure can be obtained by computing the ratio of current-account credit extended by the banks to total credit extended by the banks or the banks' "Mittelbereitstellung" in Eistert's terminology.[2] The use of this ratio makes it possible to measure the credit-constant total effect, since the ratio has been corrected for the level of total credit. If changes in this ratio can be related in a significant way to changes in the level on non-agricultural output, then a good estimate can

---

[1]This latter case is what was encountered in our empirical section where it was found that in our complete model the coefficients of labor and capital of the production function summed to more than one in contrast to our simple model where they summed to one. In the section "A Test of the Implications of our Findings" we subject our finding to an additional test suggested by Fogel and Engerman to filter out the scale effect from the credit-constant total effect.

[2]Eistert, p. 33 ff. It should be noted that the use of Mittelbereitstellung as the denominator of this fraction indicates a concern only with the allocation of credit by the banks and not with the borrowing decisions of firms.

be made of the degree of stimulus or restraint that the German non-agricultural economy received from the banks as a consequence of bank financing. A remaining question to be answered is whether the appropriate econometric test is the estimation of a cross section or time series production function.

The Appropriateness of Cross Section versus Time Series Analysis

Although it might at first appear that the correct way to approach the question of the impact of the institutional arrangements of the banking system in advancing or retarding growth in Germany in the period 1883 to 1913 is to estimate a cross sectional production function, this approach does not answer the question. We accept the testimony of Gerschenkron and others that banks made long-term loans to industry at short-term rates via current account.[1] The implication of the use of this technique is that the rate of return on long-term capital is not uniform throughout the country. The resulting substitution effect means that certain light industries used relative less capital than they should have. The problem with this approach is that it does not correct for technological change and innovation in the different industries that could account for the presumed differences in the measured marginal product of capital in these sectors. Rather than a cross section approach what is called for is a time series production function in which the ratio of current-account to total bank credit is used as a shift parameter. If the banks actually contributed to the growth of Germany in this period, then this shift parameter would enter with a positive sign.

---

[1] Gerschenkron, p. 14.

Were the converse true, this shift parameter would enter with a negative sign. The question at issue is not whether the use of current-account financing favored the growth of German heavy industry in the period. Jeidels and others noted that it did and the government could not have been expected to object to a bank policy that would have enhanced German military potential and increased the German share of world export markets.[1] The central question remains whether the policy of the banks resulted in so serious a misallocation of capital that the potential total of German non-agricultural output in the period was not reached. It is to this latter question that we address ourselves below.

Model and Data

In this section a model is developed to measure whether credit extended through current-accounts was allocated in a manner that maximized non-agricultural output. If MB is defined as the total credit extended for productive purposes by these banks, then

(1) $$MB = CA - DB + FB + SEC$$

where CA = current-account credit

DB = domestic bill credit

FB = foreign bill credit

SEC = credit extended through security holdings[2]

Since CA/MB represents the proportion of total bank credit extended through current-accounts, CA/MB serves as a proxy for the closeness

---

[1]Jeidels, p. 270. For an account of government policy toward industry in defense related matters see Eckart Kehr, _Schlachtflottenbau und Parteipolitik, 1894-1901_ (Berlin: Verlag von Emil Ebering, 1930).

[2]All the above data come from Eistert. See Appendix for a complete listing of data sources.

of the relations between these banks and industry. If, in fact, this arrangement contributed to the efficiency of the economic system, some form of CA/MB should enter into the production function as a positive shift parameter. This formulation does not test whether increases (decreases) in bank credit increase (decrease) efficiency. Rather it tests the hypothesis that a relative rise of current-account accompanied increases in efficiency.

To perform this test, we estimate a Cobb-Douglas production function with some form of CA/MB as a shift parameter.[1] The Cobb-Douglas form of the production function has been selected because it is simple and widely used. The Kmenta test has confirmed its appropriateness.[2] Specifically we postulate that

$$(2) \qquad Y = Ae^{\lambda_1 V_1 + \lambda_2 V_2 + \ . \ . \ . \ + \lambda_n V_n} L^{\alpha_1} K^{\alpha_2} u \qquad \text{where}^3$$

---

[1] It is important to note that it is not being argued that some form of CA/MB is a factor of production. Instead it is being asserted that CA/MB measures the current-account segment of total bank credit extended to industry for productive purposes. By looking at the sign of the coefficient of this shift parameter, one may determine whether an increase or a decrease in CA/MB is associated with an increase or decrease in the efficiency with which the factors of production (i.e., labor and capital) are used.

[2] To test whether the appropriate specification of the production function is Cobb-Douglas, a modification of the Kmenta test suggested by Nadiri (see M. Nadiri, "Some Approaches to the Theory and Measurement of Total Factor Productivity: A Survey," Journal of Economic Literature, VIII [December 1970], 1137-1178) pp. 1150-1154 has been used. What is required is the estimation of

$$\ell n Y = \ell n \gamma + \mu\delta \, \ell n[K/L] + \mu \ell n L + B[\ell n(K/L)]^2 + u$$

where $B = \rho\mu\delta \ (1-\delta)/2$, ρ is a substituion parameter, γ a scale parameter, δ a distribution coefficient and μ the degree of returns to scale. If B is insignificant with $\mu\delta$ significant, this indicates that $\rho=0$ which means that the elasticity of substitution $\sigma=1$ since $\sigma=1/(1+\rho)$. This would indicate

Y = real output

L = labor

K = capital

A = efficiency parameter

α_1 = elasticity of output with respect to labor

α_2 = elasticity of output with respect to capital

V_i = shift parameter $i = 1, n$

λ_i = coefficient of shift parameter $i = 1, n$

u = disturbance term

---

that the Cobb-Douglas production function is the correct specification. The results of the test are

$$\ell nY = \underset{(-3.34)}{-.04176} + \underset{(4.40)}{.5793}\ \ell n(K/L) + \underset{(10.42)}{1.462}\ \ell nL + \underset{(.356)}{.03704}\ [\ell n(K/L)]^2$$

$$R^2 = .997;\ SEE = .01618;\ DW = .747$$

where R^2 = the coefficient of determination, SEE = the standard error of the regression, DW = the Durbin-Watson statistic, and t-statistics are listed under the coefficients. Since the Durbin-Watson test indicated serial correlation of the residuals which bias the standard errors of the regression coefficients, generalized least squares has been used resulting in

$$\ell nY = \underset{(-.1720)}{-.005253} + \underset{(2.514)}{.3426}\ \ell n(K/L) + \underset{(0.789)}{1.491}\ \ell nL + \underset{(1.682)}{.3041}\ [\ell n(K/L)]^2$$

$$R^2 = .990;\ SEE = .03059;\ DW = 1.96$$

which no longer shows serial correlation of the residuals. In both equations B is insignificant at the 90% level (since the t-statistic is below 1.704) indicating that the Cobb-Douglas production function is the correct specification. μ is 1.491 which suggests increasing returns to scale. In subsequent empirical results (see Table 1) when time is added to the equation the indicated returns to scale fall substantially to a value of around unity. Data for K, L and Y are for non-agricultural output in the period 1883-1913. K and L have been corrected for utilization. For a more complete description see the data section of this paper and the Appendix on data sources.

[3]See Appendix for a complete description of data sources which are all yearly averages.

If V_1 = time, then λ_1 = the rate of disembodied or neutral technological change. If V_2 = CA/MB, then a significantly positive (negative) λ_2 indicates that as the current-account segment of total bank credit increases this will result in an increase (decrease) in the level of efficiency in the economy. This methodology allows us to measure what Gerschenkron calls the "costs of substitution," and what we call the <u>credit-constant total effect</u>.

Equation (2) is initially estimated in log linear form as

$$\text{(3)} \qquad \ell nY = \ell nA + \lambda_1 V_1 + \lambda_2 V_2 + \ldots + \lambda_n V_n + \alpha_1 \ell nL + \alpha_2 \ell nK + \ell nu.$$

using ordinary least squares. When a low Durbin-Watsun test statistic indicated serial correlation of the residuals equation (3) was reestimated with generalized least squares to obtain unbiased estimates of the standard errors of the coefficients.

Sources for Y, L and K are listed in the Appendix. Y, L and K have been corrected to reflect only non-agricultural output. We have made this correction because we note that the banks did not make loans to the agricultural sector during the period. The Gerschenkron hypothesis is that the banks significantly increased growth of heavy industry. If we were to use only data for heavy industry, such a restricted definition of output, labor and capital would not have allowed us to test whether in fact such a bias in favor of heavy industry lowered aggregate non-agricultural output. The rationale behind using non-agricultural output rather than total output is our wish to make our test more sensitive by isolating the non-agricultural sector of the economy.

Labor and capital data have been additionally corrected for

utilization using an adjustment to take into account the declining work-hours per year during the period and the rate of unemployment. It has been assumed that the rate of unemployment of labor was the same as the rate of unemployment of capital. Since Meinert's[1] data indicate that work-hours per year declined .53% each year during the period, the corrected labor value is given by

(4) $$L_i = L_i^* (.9947)^i \qquad i = 1, 31$$ where

L_i = the corrected labor figure in period i and L_i^* = raw labor figure for non-agricultural production in period i. If u_i = Kuczynski's figure for unemployment in period i[2] then

(5) $$K_i = K_i^* (1-u_i) \qquad i = 1, 31$$ where

K_i is the corrected capital figure in period i and K_i^* is the raw capital figure for non-agricultural production in period i.

Time has been added to the equation to compensate for possible adjustments in the data that cannot be measured directly because of lack of precise knowledge about changes in the quality of factors of production. It is important to test whether CA/MB replaces time or whether each or neither is significant. If time replaces CA/MB or only one shift parameter

---

[1] See R. Meinert, Die Entwicklung der Arbeitszeit in der deutschen Industrie, 1820-1956,(dissertation Münster, 1958), p. 110.

[2] Four observations for unemployment were missing in J. Kuczynski's ("Germany 1800 to the Present Day," A Short History of Labor Conditions under Industrial Capitalism, Volume III, Part I [London: Frederick Muller, Ltd., 1945]) series. These figures were generated by the use of a Phillips curve. (See A. Phillips, "The Relationship Between Unemployment and the Rate of Change of Money Wage Rates in the United Kingdom, 1861-1957," Econometrica, XXV [1958], 283-300.)

enters, this result indicates that both are a proxy for the same shift. If both enter, then it can be concluded that both measure distinct production function shifts. If neither enters, it can be concluded that our data for labor and capital are corrected completely and that there has been no shift in the production function in the period. The use of CA/MB allows us to test whether there has been any shift in the efficiency of labor and capital in the period that is due <u>only</u> to the actions of the banks in extending increasing percentages of their credit in the form of current-account credit. For definitions of the variables see the text and the Appendix. All equations have been estimated using generalized least squares with a first order lag scheme. R^2_{or} is the coefficient of determination for equation <u>not</u> corrected for autocorrelation. SEE_{or} is the standard error of estimate for equation <u>not</u> corrected for autocorrelation. The generalized least squares technique that has been used is outlined in Johnston.[1]

---

[1]For a complete discussion of the generalized least squares technique see J. Johnston, <u>Econometric Models</u> (New York: McGraw Hill Book Co., 1963), pp. 179-200. This technique involves first estimating $Y_t = a + BX_t + u_t$ to obtain a vector of errors $(u_1 \ldots u_t)$ to be used to estimate ρ where $u_t = \rho u_{t-1} + e_t$. The original equation is lagged one period, multiplied by ρ and this transformed equation subtracted from the original equation. The transformed data is then used to reestimate the original equation which is now in the form $(Y_t - \rho Y_{t-1}) = a(1-\rho) + B(X_t - \rho X_{t-1}) + e_t$. This procedure will not change the estimated coefficients. If it raises the Durbin-Watson test statistic, it will give better estimates of the standard errors of the coefficients. An alternative estimation procedure is to use first differences. This technique is merely a special case of generalized least squares where it is assumed that $\rho=1$. When Y and X are in log form, such a procedure reduces to estimating the equation in percentage change rather than in level form.

Results

Table 1 lists the results of estimating equation (2) in the form of equation (3) for various combinations of shift parameters. Equation (6) represents the usual production function with time as a shift parameter. All variables are significant and the coefficients are of the expected sign and magnitude. If our hypothesis is correct, then the results of subsequent equations will be better than those in this equation. Equation (7) replaces time with CA/MB lagged one period. The SEE of the original version of equation (7) (.0144) is lower than the SEE of the original version of equation (6) (.0151) indicating that equation (7) is a better fit. CA/MB has been lagged one period to test whether changes in the financial structure influence the economy with a lag. The highly significant negative coefficient of $(CA/MB)_{t-1}$ of -.1921 suggests that the effect of increasing the role of the Kreditbanken through current-account financing was to reduce the efficiency of the economy after a one year lag. Equation (7) indicates increasing returns to scale on the order of what was found when the Kmenta test was run. This result appears to be a consequence of omitting time from equation (7). Equation (8) rectifies this omission by including both $(CA/MB)_{t-1}$ and time. Both variables are significant and indicate that while there was positive neutral technological change in the economy the effect of increased bank credit via current-account was a reduction in potential output. Because of the inclusion of time, the measured degree of increasing returns to scale falls. In equation (8) the SEE of the original equation falls still further to .0128. Equation (9) adds CA/MB and $(CA/MB)_{t-2}$ to equation (7). These terms do not enter significantly suggesting that the effect of changes

TABLE 1

ESTIMATES OF THE PARAMETERS OF THE COBB-DOUGLAS PRODUCTION FUNCTION, GERMANY 1883-1913

(6) $$\ell nY = \underset{(5.45)}{-.06322} + \underset{(3.053)}{.01562T} + \underset{(1.996)}{.2533\ell nK} + \underset{(3.556)}{.7443\ell nL}$$

$R^2_{or} = .998$; $SEE_{or} = .0151$; $R^2 = .996$; See = .0232; DW = 1.79; $\alpha_1 + \alpha_2 = .9976$

(7) $$\ell nY = \underset{(1.42)}{.0542} - \underset{(-2.96)}{.1921(CA/MB)_{t-1}} + \underset{(6.69)}{.5762\ell nK} + \underset{(4.85)}{1.011\ell nL}$$

$R^2_{or} = .998$; $SEE_{or} = .0144$; $R^2 = .991$; SEE = .0293; DW = 1.86; $\alpha_1 + \alpha_2 = 1.5872$

(8) $$\ell nY = \underset{(.4753)}{.01754} + \underset{(2.57)}{.01187T} - \underset{(-2.31)}{.1429(CA/MB)_{t-1}} + \underset{(2.93)}{.3485\ell nK} + \underset{(3.99)}{.8070\ell nL}$$

$R^2_{or} = .9985$; $SEE_{or} = .0128$; $R^2 = .994$; SEE = .0245; DW = 1.87; $\alpha_1 + \alpha_2 = 1.1555$

(9) $$\ell nY = \underset{(.1618)}{.0128} + \underset{(2.51)}{.0124T} \underset{(-.1255)}{-.08907(CA/MB)} - \underset{(-2.11)}{.1443(CA/MB)_{t-1}} + \underset{(.275)}{.0223\ (CA/MB)_{t-2}}$$
$$+ \underset{(2.72)}{.3559\ell nK} + \underset{(2.97)}{.7482\ell nL}$$

$R^2_{or} = .999$; $SEE_{or} = .0131$; $R^2 = .996$; SEE = .0216; DW = 1.67; $\alpha_1 + \alpha_2 = 1.1041$

(10) $$\ell nY = \underset{(.682)}{.0561} + \underset{(1.90)}{.009748T} - \underset{(-.407)}{.02826(CA/MB)} - \underset{(-2.65)}{.1883(CA/MB)_{t-1}} + \underset{(.4238)}{.0334(CA/MB)_{t-2}}$$
$$+ \underset{(3.28)}{.4828\ell nK} + \underset{(2.30)}{.6063\ell nL}$$

$R^2 = .996$; SEE = .0196; DW = 1.84; $\alpha_1 + \alpha_2 = 1.0891$

t-statistics under coefficients.

in the structure of the banking system is not instantaneous. Time and $(CA/MB)_{t-1}$ remain significant and are unaffected by the inclusion of these two variables. Since the Durbin-Watson test for equation (9) is right on the boundary, a second order generalized least squares scheme has been used to estimate equation (10). This procedure does not alter our results which show conclusively that the role of the banks in allocating current-account credit was to decrease the efficienty of the economy. In an additional equation not reported, $(CA/MB)_{t-3}$ and $(CA/MB)_{t-4}$ have been added to equation (9) to test whether other lagged values of CA/MB enter significantly. Their failure to do so gives us further confidence in our interpretation of the negative coefficient of $(CA/MB)_{t-1}$.

A Further Verification of the Hypothesis

Although the analysis of the preceding section gives convincing evidence that the role of the banks in allocating current-account credit was to reduce the efficiency of the economy, there is some question as to how a negative coefficient of $(CA/MB)_{t-1}$ should be interpreted. It is possible that it is not increases in CA that cause a negative coefficient but instead increases in MB. Were this the case, it would imply an entirely different hypothesis. In order to test this hypothesis we estimated an equation where $(CA/MB)_{t-1}$ was replaced by $\ell n(CA/P)_{t-1}$ and $\ell n(MB/P)_{t-1}$, where P is the price index. This equation does not argue that these variables should be treated in inputs in the production function; rather, it uses them only to test which variable retains significance. The results listed below show that while $\ell n(MB/P)_{t-1}$ is not significant

(11)
$$\ell nY = -.02298 + .01262t + .3383\ell nK + .8335\ell nL$$
$$(1.057) \quad (2.41) \quad (2.66) \quad (3.91)$$
$$+ .07658\ell n(MB/P)_{t-1} - .08695\ell n(CA/P)_{t-1}$$
$$(1.41) \quad (-2.04)$$
$$R^2_{or} = .9986;\ SEE_{or} = .01259;\ R^2 = .995;\ SEE = .02259;\ DW = 1.76$$

show that while $\ell n(MB/P)_{t-1}$ is not significant $\ell n(CA/P)_{t-1}$ is negatively significant. This evidence confirms our prior conclusion that the role of the Kreditbanken in allocating current-account credit was to inhibit growth. As a further verification, $\ell n(MB/P)_{t-1}$ has been added to equation (9). These results listed in equation (12) below further support our hypothesis.[1]

(12)
$$\ell nY = .09968 + .01294t + .3361\ell nK + .8156\ell nL$$
$$(.4918) \quad (2.50) \quad (2.65) \quad (3.82)$$
$$- .1371(CA/MB)_{t-1} - .09843\ell n(MB/P)_{t-1}$$
$$(-2.05) \quad (-.4095)$$
$$R^2_{or} = .9987;\ SEE_{or} = .01249;\ R^2 = .995;\ SEE = .0225;\ DW = 1.79$$

In equation (12) $(CA/MB)_{t-1}$ remains significant even when $\ell n(MB/P)_{t-1}$ is added to the equation. This result proves that the negative coefficients that are reported for $(CA/MB)_{t-1}$ in equation (7), (8), (9) and (10) are not due to an increase of $(MB/P)_{t-1}$. This finding shows that $(CA/MB)_{t-1}$ is a valid shift parameter to test whether in allocating current-account credit the banks added to the efficiency of the economy in the period 1883-1913.

At this time it is important to note that we are not making a

---

[1]Both equation (11) and (12) have been estimated using generalized least squares with a first order lag scheme.

cyclical argument for $(CA/MB)_{t-1}$ being significant. If such an argument were made, it would proceed in the following fashion. If we argue that the banks converted current-account loans to long-term debt or equity then, CA might fall in periods of high growth of output, since in such periods it was easier to sell long-term securities. There are several problems with this argument. First, if this argument holds, then MB would have fallen when CA fell and in that case we should find CA and MB highly collinear. This result is not what is shown by equation (11) where we note that $\ell n(CA/P)_{t-1}$ remains significant in the presence of $\ell n(MB/P)_{t-1}$. Another problem with this cyclical argument is that it is not consistent with the persistent rise in CA/MB over the period despite the positive significance of time. What occurred was an increase in the percentage of MB that was CA during the period. If the cyclical argument were consistent with a positive coefficient on time, one should find that there were cyclical fluctuations about a constant mean "long-term" value of CA/MB. This pattern is not what the data show.

Another possible variant of the cyclical argument is to assert that during periods of high growth other categories of credit such as domestic bill credit and foreign bill credit increased lowering the level of $(CA/MB)_{t-1}$ and giving us our result. The problem with this interpretation is that it is not consistent with the evidence in equations (11) and (12) which indicates that $\ell n(MB)_{t-1}$ does not enter the equation significantly when either $(CA/MB)_{t-1}$ or $\ell n(CA/P)_{t-1}$ is in the equation.

A Test of the Implications of Our Findings

While our findings show that the increased role of the Kreditbanken in current-account financing tended to reduce the efficiency of the economy at some levels of output by lowering the intercept of the production function, a close inspection of our results indicates that the measured returns to scale increased from essentially one (.9976, to be exact) in equation (6) to some value more than one in equations (7) to (10).[1] These findings suggest that the banks caused some form of increasing returns to scale, oligopolistic market structure. An interesting question is whether the resulting scale effect arising from the level of operation of these new industrial facilities was large enough to overcome the inefficiences introduced by the apparent misallocation of current-account credit. Fogel and Engerman have suggested a test to determine whether the economy was actually operating at a level high enough to overcome (via increasing returns) the reduction of the intercept of the production function. This test[2] reduced to whether ξ is greater or less than one where

---

[1]The measured returns to scale can be calculated by adding the coefficients of labor and capital (α_1 and α_2).

[2]For a complete discussion of this test see R. Fogel and S. Engerman, Time on the Cross: The Economics of American Negro Slavery (Boston: Little, Brown and Co., 1973), Appendix B. The essential idea is to rewrite

A $\quad Y = \hat{A}L^{\alpha_1}K^{\alpha_2}$ $\quad$ as

B $\quad Y = \hat{A}[Y/A]^{\beta/(1+\beta)}\ L^{(\alpha_1/1+\beta)}\ K^{(\alpha_2/1+\beta)}$

In order to do this we must develop coefficients X_1 and X_2 such that

(13) $$\xi = [\hat{A}'/\hat{A}]\ [y'/\hat{A}']^{\beta/1+\beta}$$

and it is assumed that the base equation has constant returns to scale

and Y' is the mean of output

$\hat{A}'$ is the intercept of the equation to be tested

$\hat{A}$ is the intercept of the base equation

$\beta = \alpha_1 + \alpha_2 - 1$

C $$\alpha_1/(1+\beta) + X_1 = \alpha_1 \text{ and } \alpha_2/(1+\beta) + X_2 = \alpha_2$$

then reduce to $X_1 = \beta\alpha_1/(1+\beta)$ and $X_2 = \beta\alpha_2/(1+\beta)$

we can now rewrite equation A as

D $$Y = \hat{A}L^{\alpha_1/(1+\beta)}K^{\alpha_2/(1+\beta)}L^{\beta\alpha_1(1+\beta)}K^{\beta\alpha_2/(1+\alpha)}$$

we note that

E $$L^{\beta\alpha_1/(1+\beta)}K^{\beta\alpha_2/(1+\beta)} = [Y/\hat{A}]^{\beta/1+\beta}$$

Equation D can now be quickly reduced to equation B where

F $$\hat{A}[Y/\hat{A}]^{\beta/1+\beta}$$

is the "adjusted" intercept that takes into account the effects of possible increasing (decreasing) returns to scale.

The test reduces to computing ξ which is the ratio of the two "adjusted" intercepts. The general form of ξ is

G $$\frac{\hat{A}'[Y'/\hat{A}']^{\beta/1+\beta}}{\hat{A}[Y/\hat{A}]^{\beta_o/1+\beta_o}} = \xi$$

which quickly reduced to equation (13) when the base equation has returns to scale equal to one which implies $\beta_o = 0$.

The results for ξ of such a test for equations (7), (8), (9) and (10) in comparison to equations (6) are .98, .99, .94 and .94 respectively. Since all values of ξ are less than one, these results indicate that the gains from increasing returns to scale (measured by the sum of the coefficients of labor and capital) in equation (7) to (10) did not outweigh the losses of output due to the shift downward of the production function measured by the negative coefficient on the shift parameter $(CA/MB)_{t-1}$. This test shows that the scale of operations of the German non-agricultural economy in the period 1883 to 1913 was apparently not large enough to overcome the downshift in the production function that resulted from the increasing use of current-account credit by the banks.[1]

An Alternative Specification of the Model

We have presented arguments in support of the hypothesis that the industrial financing of the Kreditbanken was plagued by an allocative inefficiency serious enough to have limited the growth on non-agricultural output. The preceding section on the Fogel and Engerman test was based

---

[1]The Fogel-Engerman test uses the mean values of all variables within the sample period. While this procedure is correct, the use of the technique does not answer the question, will the scale effect ever outweigh the static efficiency loss within the sample period? To answer this question, we have computed ξ for equations (7), (8), (9) and (10) in comparison to equation (6) where we have used end of sample period values for all variables. The values of ξ are .94, .97, .90 and .89 respectively, which are uniformly lower than those obtained for ξ when the mean values of these variables were used. The explanation is that during the sample period the rise in CA/MB was sufficient to outweigh the increase in production arising from the measured increasing returns to scale. If the level of CA/MB had remained constant, then the increasing returns might eventually have "cancelled" the output reducing effect of the static loss associated with CA/MB.

on the belief that in some fashion the actions of the Kreditbanken were captured by an increase in the measured returns to scale in equations (7) through (10) in comparison to equation (6). Such an interpretation may be overly generous to the Gerschenkron view since it is equally plausible to argue that the level of increasing returns to scale as measured in an equation such as (8) or (9) more nearly reflects a true measure of the returns to scale because the returns to scale as measured in equation (6) are downwardly biased owing to incompleteness of the model. In this section we test this hypothesis by restructuring the model so that constant returns to scale are assumed. In this manner we obtain a measure of the effect of the method of industrial financing by the Kreditbanken.

If we assume that $\alpha_1 + \alpha_2 = 1$, then equation (2) becomes

$$(14) \qquad Y/L = Ae^{\lambda_1 V_1 + \lambda_2 V_2 + \ldots + \lambda_n V_n} [K/L]^{\alpha_1}$$

which can be estimated in log-linear form. Such estimates are presented in equation (15) and (16), where we have used GLS because the original equations indicated serial correlation.

$$(15) \qquad \ell n(Y/L) = \underset{(.3571)}{.01281} + \underset{(5.71)}{.01481T} - \underset{(-2.20)}{.1309}(CA/MB)_{t-1} + \underset{(2.840)}{.3218}\ell n(K/L)$$

$$SEE_{or} = .01256; \; SEE = .02342; \; R^2 = .98; \; DW = 1.885$$

$$(16) \qquad \ell n(Y/L) = \underset{(4.764)}{.01397T} - \underset{(=3.399)}{.1374}(CA/MB)_{t-1} + \underset{(.736)}{.03567}(CA/MB)_{t-2} + \underset{(2.963)}{.3473}\ell n(K/L)$$

$$SEE_{or} = .01299; \; SEE = .0200; \; R^2 = .988; \; DW = 1.65$$

Equation (15) supports our hypothesis that the actions of the <u>Kreditbanken</u> lowered potential output since the coefficient of $(CA/MB)_{t-1}$ is negatively significant. Equation (16) shows similar results, although not all the variables entered the equation due to insufficient F-level.[1] The alternative specification of the model shows that our results are not sensitive to the assumption of non-constant returns to scale. It is interesting to note that although in equation (15) in comparison to equation (8) the coefficient of time is biased upward owing to the constraint of $\alpha_1 + \alpha_2 = 1$, $(CA/MB)_{t-1}$ remains highly significant.[2] Thus although equation (8), (9) and (10) are probably better specifications of the underlying production function in the period, our findings are not sensitive to our not assuming constant returns to scale.

<u>Conclusion</u>

Since the sign of the coefficient of the shift parameter in this model is a proxy for the efficiency of allocation of current-account credit and in every case the coefficient was negatively significant for this shift parapmeter lagged one period, it can be concluded from this model that the industrial financing of the <u>Kreditbanken</u> in the period 1883 to 1913 was plagued by serious allocative inefficiency. Such

---

[1] In equation (16) the constant and CA/MB would not enter.

[2] If the coefficient on time was the same in equation (8) and (15) this would suggest that there actually were constant returns to scale and that the estimates of α_1 and α_2 in equation (8) were biased upward. Our contrary finding suggests that in fact it is a misspecification to assume constant returns to scale and that α_1 and α_2 are not biased in equation (8).

inefficiency caused German non-agricultural output to remain substantially beneath the level of output that might have been attained. Given the financial acumen of Kreditbank directors, one doubts that this result was accidental. Rather, it seems more likely that this result was caused by a conscious and broadly shared bias. As has been noted earlier, Alexander Gerschenkron and Otto Jeidels, a contemporary scholar and banker, call attention to the banks' bias in favor of heavy industry and against light industry.[1] This bias might have reflected nothing more than bankers' own priorities or tastes. It is not inconceivable that acting on their own, the banks could have enforced a generally accepted ordering of priorities on the entire non-agricultural economy; but, such a view raises additional questions.

Would such a bank policy have met with sufficient support among those whose views counted in such matters? There would, of course, have been no objections from the chief beneficiaries, the leaders of heavy industry. The government also had little reason to object to such a bank policy and some quite persuasive grounds for tolerating or even encouraging the banks to act as they seem to have acted. The prominence of heavy industrial products among German exports was known to all. Furthermore, the Prussian bureaucracy had an acute sensitivity to and concern for the military implications of the policies upon which it passed judgment. That a strong heavy industrial sector was a potent factor in military calculations hardly requires explanation. Under these circumstances it is not possible to say with certainty whether the banks

---

[1] Gerschenkron, p. 15 and Jeidels, p. 270.

were pursuing this policy autonomously or in cooperation with industry and government. The most likely explanation of the banks' policy is that it represented but one aspect of a common outlook that bankers shared with major industrialists and government leaders alike. Assuming that this policy resulted from such agreement, these men surely knew the policy's benefits. How many knew its cost?[1]

---

[1] It is interesting to speculate how much loss on non-agricultural output was actually associated with the rise of the use of the current-account by the banks. If we assume that -.1429 is the coefficient of $(CA/MB)_{t-1}$ (see equation (8)) and that the index number on non-agricultural output in 1913 was 3.010300778, the rise in CA/MB from 50.8% to 72.8% in the period caused an apparent loss of real output of .093165691. The percentage loss was 3.1%.

CHAPTER V

SUMMARY AND CONCLUSION

In examining the role of German banks in the development of the German economy from 1870 to 1914, two different approaches have been taken. The two main types of financial institutions active in Germany in this era, private banks and Kreditbanken, have been observed and analyzed using archival materials relating to each type. In addition, an econometric model has been used to analyze the Kreditbanken. Each approach adds to our understanding of the banks' role in a way that the other cannot. Together they provide a useful account of the role of the German banks from 1870 to 1914.

The role of the private bank is explored in a discussion of Gebruder Bethmann of Frankfurt am Main. Private banks like Gebruder Bethmann were primarily engaged in commercial and state finance. By aiding commerce and contributing to the development of a modern capital market, the private banks played an important part in German economic development. The contribution of these banks, especially that in fostering commerce, made industrialization easier than it otherwise would have been. Nonetheless, the direct contribution of most private banks to industrialization was quite limited. When commerce began to yield its place to industry after 1850, private bankers recognized that a new type of institution was required and assisted in the formation of *Kreditbanken* while continuing their own operations in the more traditional fields. Until 1914 commerce continued to benefit from the services of private banks, but industrial development was supported largely by *Kreditbanken* and only to a limited extent by private banks.

The role of the *Kreditbank* is investigated in a discussion of the Deutsche Bank. Here can be seen the advantages of the joint-stock form in allowing the establishment of large financial institutions engaged in both investment and commercial banking. Those most in need of the services of the *Kreditbanken* were the newly developing industries of Germany after 1850. By providing those services, the *Kreditbanken* became active participants in the industrialization of Germany. They worked closely with industrial entrepreneurs and managers in finance and often in other fields of the firms' decision making as well. The prestige and financial strength of the *Kreditbanken* gave bankers considerable influence among industrialists, an influence that was reflected in the many directorships bankers held on industrial boards of directors. Evidence regarding the extent and character of such influence has been offered in this discussion of the Deutsche Bank. A comprehensive understanding of what use the banks made of their influence and what resulted for the German economy as a whole could not be obtained from the available archives.

A step toward obtaining such an understanding has been taken with the formulation of an econometric model of the German non-agricultural economy for the years 1883 to 1913. Because current-account credit was the vehicle by which most *Kreditbank* credit was extended to industry, the ratio of current-account credit to total *Kreditbank* credit has been incorporated into a production function as a shift parameter. Statistical tests show that this ratio has been used appropriately. The sign of the coefficient of this ratio is negative indicating that the Kreditbanken allocated credit in a manner that reduced the efficiency of the German non-agricultural economy. In this way some measure of the influence of the Kreditbanken on the German non-agricultural economy between 1883 and 1913 has been obtained.

It is possible that this loss of efficiency occurred because the Kreditbanken followed credit allocation policies that were biased in favor of heavy and against light industry or in favor of export and defense industries. The archives presently available to American scholars offer no conclusive answer to this question. The most that can be said on the basis of available archival evidence is that the existence of such biases cannot be ruled out. This question merits further investigation when the relevant source materials become available.

APPENDIX

DEFINITIONS OF VARIABLES AND SOURCES OF DATA

OUTPUT: real NNP for non-agricultural sector = real NNP at factor cost = agricultural product at factor cost (1913 prices), Hoffman (pp. 454-455, cols. 10 and 1 respectively).

LABOR: labor force in non-agricultural sector = total employment, Hoffman (p. 205, col. 9) = agricultural work force, Hoffman, (p. 205, col. 1). This raw figure was adjusted via equation (4) using Meinert's data (p. 110) on work-hours per year.

CAPITAL: capital in non-agricultural sector = total capital stock derived from Hoffman (p. 26, col. 2) times the percentage of capital stock that is not agricultural derived from Hoffman (p. 44). Thus, quantity is adjusted for utilization via equation (5) using Kuczynski's data (p. 163) on unemployment.

PRICE: derived from dividing nominal output, Hoffmann (p. 248, col. 5), by real output, Hoffman (p. 827, col. 7).

CA: current-account credit, Eistert (Table 15, p. 98).

DB: domestic bill credit, Eistert (p. 82, col. 7a).

FB: foreign bill credit, Eistert (p. 120, col. 3).

SEC: credit extended through securities, Eistert (Table 19-21, col. 6).

Where Hoffmann refers to W. Hoffmann, _Das Wachstum der deutschen Wirtschaft seit der Mitte des 19. Janrhunderts_ (Berlin: Springer Verlag, 1965) and Eistert refer to E. Eistert, _Die Beeinflussung des Wirtschaftswachstums in Deutschland von 1883 bis 1913 durch das Bankensystem_ (Berlin: Duncker & Humblot, 1970). Meinert refers to R. Meinert, _Die Entwicklung der Arbeitszeit in der deutschen Industrie, 1820-1956_, Dissertation, Münster, 1958. Note that the above data are annual averages.

BIBLIOGRAPHY

Books and Dissertations

Barkin, Kenneth D. The Controversy over German Industrialization, 1890-1902. Chicago: University of Chicago Press, 1970.

Bosenick, Alfred. Neudeutsche gemischte Bankwirtschaft. Berlin: J. Schweitzer Verlag, 1912.

Bosselmann, Kurt. Die Entwicklung des deutschen Aktienwesens im 19. Jahrhundert. Berlin: Walter de Gruyter and Co., 1939.

Cameron, Rondo (ed.). Banking and Economic Development. New York: Oxford University Press, 1972.

__________. France and the Economic Development of Europe. Chicago: Rand, McNally, 1966.

Clapham, J.H. The Economic Development of France and Germany, 1815-1914. Cambridge, U.K.: Cambridge University Press, 1963.

Eberstadt, Rudolph. Der deutsche Kapitalmarkt. Leipzig: Duncker und Humblot, 1901.

Eistert, Ekkehard. Die Beeinflussung des Wirtschaftswachstums in Deutschland von 1883 bis 1913 durch das Bankensystem. Berlin: Duncker und Humblot, 1970.

Fasolt, F. Die sieben grössten Elektrizitätsgesellschaften, ihre Entwicklung und Unternehmehertätigkeit. Dresden, 1904.

Fogel, R. W. and Engerman, S. L. Time of the Cross: The Economics of American Negro Slavery. Boston: Little, Brown, 1974.

Gehr, Martin. "Das Verhältnis zwischen Banken und Industrie in Deutschland seit der Mitte des 19. Jahrhunderts bis zur Bankenkrise von 1931 unter besonderer Berücksichtigung des industriellen Grosskredits." Unpublished Ph.D. dissertation, University of Tübingen, 1959.

Gerschenkron, Alexander. Economic Backwardness in Historical Perspective. Cambridge: Harvard University Press, 1962.

Hagemann, Wilhelm. Das Verhältnis der deutschen Grossbanken zur Industrie. Berlin: Christians, 1931.

Hasse, Hermann. Die Allgemeine Elektrizitäts-Gesellschaft und ihre wirtschaftliche Bedeutung. Heidelberg: Karl Winter, 1902.

Helfferich, Karl. Georg von Siemens, Ein Lebensbild aus Deutschlands grosser Zeit. Berlin: Julius Springer, 1923.

Heyn, Udo. "Private Banking and Industrialization: The Case of Frankfurt am Main, 1825-1875." Unpublished Ph.D. dissertation, University of Wisconsin, Department of Economics, 1969.

Hilferding, Rudolph. Das Finanzkapital. Frankfurt: Europäische Verlaganstalt, 1968.

Hoffmann, Walther. Das Wachstum der deutschen Wirtschaft seit der Mitte des 19. Jahrhunderts. Berlin: Springer, 1965.

Hook, Walter. Die wirtschaftliche Entwicklung der ehemaligen Deutschen Bank in Spiegel ihrer Bilanzen. Heidelberg: Karl Winter, 1954.

Huth, Walter. Die Entwicklung der deutschen and französischen Grossbanken im Zusammenhange mit der Entwicklung der Nationalwirtschaft. Berlin: Siemenroth, 1918.

Johnston, J. Econometric Methods. New York: Mc-Graw-Hill, 1963.

Karnath, Kurt. "Über die Stellung der Kreditbanken zur Industrie." Unpublished Ph.D. dissertation, University of Frankfurt, 1924.

Kehr, Eckart. Schlachtflottenbau und Parteipolitik, 1884-1901. Berlin: Verlag von Emil Ebering, 1930.

Kirchholtes, H. Jüdische Privatbanken in Frankfurt am Main. Frankfurt: Verlag von Waldemar Kramer, 1969.

Kuczynski, Jürgen. A Short History of Labour Conditions Under Industrial Capitalism, Vol. III, Part I. London: Frederick Muller, Ltd., 1945.

Landes, David. The Unbound Prometheus. Cambridge, U.K.: Cambridge University Press, 1969.

Luke, Rolf. Die Berliner Handelsgesellschaft in einem Jahrhundert deutschen Wirtschaft. Berlin: Bruder Hartmann, 1956.

Marx, Karl. Capital. Chicago: Charles H. Kerr and Co., 1909.

Mauersberg, Hans. Deutsche Industrien im Zeitgeschehen eines Jahrhunderts. Stuttgart: Gustave Fischer Verlag, 1966.

Meinert, Ruth. "Die Entwicklung der Arbeitszeit in der deutschen Industrie, 1820-1956." Unpublished Ph.D. dissertation, University of Münster, 1958.

Model, Paul. *Die grossen Berliner Effektenbanken*. Jena: Verlag von Gustav Fischer, 1896.

National Monetary Commission. *Miscellaneous Articles on German Banking*. Washington: Government Printing Office, 1910.

__________. *The Reichsbank, 1876-1900*. Washington: Government Printing Office, 1910.

Plenge, Johann. *Von der Diskontpolitik zer Herrschaft über den Geldmarkt*. Berlin: Julius Springer, 1913.

Riesser, Jacob. *Zur Entwicklungsgeschichte der deutschen Grossbanken mit besonderer Rücksicht auf die Konzentrationsbestrebungen*. Jena: Verlag von Gustav Fischer, 1906.

__________. *The Great German Banks and their Concentration*. Washington: Government Printing Office, 1911.

Sattler, Heinrich. *Die Effektbanken*. Leipzig: Karl Winter, 1890.

Schulze-Gaevernitz, Gerhard von. *Grundriss der Sozialökonomik, V Abteilung, II Teil. Die deutsche Kreditbank*. Tübingen: Mohr, 1922.

Schumpeter, Joseph. *Business Cycles*. New York: McGraw-Hill, 1939.

Seidenzahl, Fritz. *100 Jahre Deutsche Bank 1870-1970*. Frankfurt: Johannes Weisbecker, 1970.

Sombart, Werner. *Das Wirtschaftsleben im Zeitalter des Hochkapitalismus*. Munich: Duncker and Humblot, 1928.

Tilly, Richard. *Financial Institutions and Industrialization in the Rhineland, 1815-1870*. Madison: University of Wisconsin Press, 1966.

Vogelstein, Theodor. *Grundriss der Sozialökonomik, VI Abteilung, II Teil. Die Finanzielle Organisation der kapitalistischen Industrie und die Monopolbildung*. Tübingen: Mohr, 1923.

Wallich, Paul. *Die Konzentration im Deutschen Bankwesen*. Berlin: J. G. Cotta'sche Buchhandlung, 1905.

Weber, Adolf. *Depositenbanken und Spekulationsbanken*. Leipzig: Duncker und Humblot, 1902.

Wolff, Siegfried. *Das Gründungsgeschäft im deutschen Bankgewerbe*. Berlin: J. G. Cotta'sche Buchhandlung, 1915.

Articles

Blumberg, Horst. "Die Finanzierung der Neugrundungen und Erweiterungen von Industriebetrieben in Form der Aktiengesellschaften während der fünfziger Jahre des 19. Jahrhunderts in Deutschland, am Beispiel der preussischen Verhältnisse erläutert," in Hans Mottek (ed.) Studien zur Geschichte der Industriellen Revolution in Deutschland. Berlin: Akademie-Verlag, 1960.

Borchardt, Knut. "Zur Frage des Kapitalmangels in der ersten Hälfte des 19. Jahrhunderts in Deutschland," Jahrbücher für Nationalökonomie und Statistik, CLXXIII (1961), 401-421.

Born, Karl Erich. "Der soziale und wirtschaftliche Strukturwandel Deutschlands am Ende des 19. Jahrhunderts," Vierteljahrschrift für Sozial- und Wirtschaftsgeschichte, L(1963), 361-376.

Cameron, Rondo. "Founding of the Bank of Darmstadt," Explorations in Entrepreneurial History, VIII, No. 3 (1956), 113-130.

Helfferich, Karl. "Der deutsche Geldmarkt 1895 bis 1902," Schriften des Verein für Sozialpolitik, VI (1903), 1-80.

Hoffmann, Walther. "Die unverteilten Gewinne der Kapitalgesellschaften 1871-1957," Zeitschrift für die Gesamte Staatswissenschaft, CXV (1959), 271-291.

Jeidels, Otto. "Das Verhältnis der deutschen Grossbanken zur Industrie mit besonderer Berücksichtigung der Eisenindustrie," Staats- und sozialwissenschaftliche Forschungen, XXII (1905), 1-271.

Kmenta, Jan. "On Estimation of the CES Production Function," International Economic Review, VIII (June 1967), 180-189.

Loeb, Ernst. "Die Berliner Grossbanken in den Jahren 1895 bis 1902 und die Krisis der Jahre 1900 und 1901," Schriften des Vereins für Sozialpolitik, VI (1903), 81-319.

Marx, Karl. "Preussen und die Hohenzollern um die Jahreswende, 1858-59," in Marx-Engels-Lenis-Stalin--Zur deutschen Geschichte. Berlin: Akademie-Verlag, 1954.

Mottek, Hans. "Zur Verstaatlichung im Kapitalismus -- der Fall Hibernia," Jahrbuch für Wirtschaftsgeschichte, IV (1968), 11-25.

Nadiri, M. I. "Some Approaches to the Theory and Measurement of Total Factor Productivity: A Survey," Journal of Economic Literature, VIII (December 1970), 1137-1178.

Phillips, A. W. "The Relationship Between Unemployment and the Rate of Change of Money Wage Rates in the United Kingdom, 1861-1957," *Economica*, XXV (1958), 283-300.

Tilly, Richard. "Soll und Haben: Recent German Economic History and the Problem of Economic Development," *Journal of Economic History*, XXX (June 1969), 298.

Zorn, Wolfgang. "Wirtschafts- und sozialgeschichtliche Zusammenhange der deutschen Reichsgründungszeit, 1850-1879," *Historische Zeitschrift*, CXCVII (1963), 318-342.

ERRATA

Page 82 line 20	"Werner von Siemens" should read "Wilhelm von Siemens"
footnote 1	"Werner von Siemens" should read "Wilhelm von Siemens"
Page 86 line 7	"Werner von Siemens" should read "Wilhelm von Siemens"
line 30	"Werner von Siemens" should read "Wilhelm von Siemens"
footnote 1	"Werner von Siemens" should read "Wilhelm von Siemens

DISSERTATIONS IN EUROPEAN ECONOMIC HISTORY

An Arno Press Collection

Atkin, John Michael. **British Overseas Investment, 1918-1931** (Doctoral Dissertation, University of London, 1968). 1977

Brosselin, Arlette. **Les Forêts De La Côte D'Or Au XIXème Siècle, et L'Utilisation De Leurs Produits** (Doctoral Thesis, Université de Dijon, 1973). 1977

Brumont, Francis. **La Bureba A L'Époque De Philippe II** (Doctoral Dissertation, Université de Toulouse, 1974). 1977

Cohen, Jon S. **Finance and Industrialization in Italy, 1894-1914** (Doctoral Dissertation, University of California, Berkeley, 1966). 1977

Dagneau, Jacques. **Les Agences Régionales Du Crédit Lyonnais, Années 1870-1914** (Doctoral Thesis, Université de Paris-VIII, 1975). 1977

Dennis, Kenneth G. **'Competition' in the History of Economic Thought** (Doctoral Dissertation, Oxford University, 1975). 1977

Desert, Gabriel. **Une Société Rurale Au XIXe Siècle:** Les Paysans Du Calvados, 1815-1895 (Doctoral Dissertation, Université de Paris, Sorbonne, 1971). 1977

Fierain, Jacques. **Les Raffineries De Sucre Des Ports En France:** XIXe -- début du XXe siècles (Doctoral Dissertation, Université de Nantes, 1974). 1977

Goreux, Louis-Marie. **Agricultural Productivity and Economic Development in France, 1852-1950** (Doctoral Dissertation, University of Chicago, 1955). With the Revised French Version. 1977

Guignet, Philippe. **Mines, Manufactures et Ouvriers Du Valenciennois Au XVIIIe Siècle** (Doctoral Dissertation, Université de Lille III, 1976). Two vols. in one. 1977

Haines, Michael R. **Economic-Demographic Interrelations in Developing Agricultural Regions:** A Case Study of Prussian Upper Silesia, 1840-1914 (Doctoral Dissertation, University of Pennsylvania, 1971). 1977

Hohorst, Gerd. **Wirtschaftswachstum Und Bevölkerungsentwicklung In Preussen 1816 Bis 1914** (Doctoral Dissertation, University of Münster, 1977). 1977

Huertas, Thomas Francis. **Economic Growth and Economic Policy in a Multinational Setting:** The Habsburg Monarchy, 1841-1865 (Doctoral Dissertation, University of Chicago, 1977). 1977

Jankowski, Manfred. **Public Policy in Industrial Growth:** The Case of the Early Ruhr Mining Region, 1766-1865 (Doctoral Dissertation, University of Wisconsin, 1969). 1977

Jefferys, James B. **Business Organisation in Great Britain, 1856-1914** (Doctoral Dissertation, University of London, 1938). 1977

Kirchhain, Günter. **Das Wachstum Der Deutschen Baumwollindustrie Im 19. Jahrhundert** (Doctoral Dissertation, University of Münster, 1973). 1977

Von Laer, Hermann. **Industrialisierung Und Qualität Der Arbeit Eine Bildungsökonomische Untersuchung Für Das 19. Jahrhundert** (Doctoral Dissertation, University of Münster, 1975). 1977

Lee, W. R. **Population Growth, Economic Development and Social Change in Bavaria, 1750-1850** (Revised Doctoral Dissertation, University of Oxford, 1972). 1977

LeVeen, E. Phillip. **British Slave Trade Suppression Policies, 1821-1865** (Doctoral Dissertation, University of Chicago, 1972). 1977

Metzer, Jacob. **Some Economic Aspects of Railroad Development in Tsarist Russia** (Doctoral Dissertation, University of Chicago, 1972). 1977

Moe, Thorvald. **Demographic Developments and Economic Growth in Norway, 1740-1940** (Doctoral Dissertation, Stanford University, 1970). 1977

Mueller, Reinhold C. **The Procuratori di San Marco and the Venetian Credit Market:** A Study of the Development of Credit and Banking in the Trecento (Doctoral Dissertation, Johns Hopkins University, 1969). 1977

Neuburger, Hugh. **German Banks and German Economic Growth from Unification to World War I** (Doctoral Dissertation, University of Chicago, 1974). 1977

Newell, William Henry. **Population Change and Agricultural Developments in Nineteenth Century France** (Doctoral Dissertation, University of Pennsylvania, 1971). 1977

Saly, Pierre. **La Politique Des Grands Travaux En France, 1929-1939** (Doctoral Dissertation, Université de Paris VIII, Vincennes, 1975). 1977

Shrimpton, Colin. **The Landed Society and the Farming Community of Essex in the Late Eighteenth and Early Nineteenth Centuries** (Doctoral Dissertation, Cambridge University, 1965). 1977

Tortella[-Casares], Gabriel. **Banking, Railroads, and Industry in Spain, 1829-1874** (Doctoral Dissertation, University of Wisconsin, 1972). 1977

Viallon, Jean-Baptiste. **La Croissance Agricole En France Et En Bourgogne De 1850 A Nos Jours** (Doctoral Dissertation, Université de Dijon, 1976). 1977

Villiers, Patrick. **Le Commerce Colonial Atlantique Et La Guerre D'Indépendance Des États Unis D'Amérique, 1778-1783** (Doctoral Dissertation, Université de Paris I, Pantheon-Sorbonne, 1975). 1977

Walters, R. H. **The Economic and Business History of the South Wales Steam Coal Industry, 1840-1914** (Doctoral Dissertation, Oxford University, 1975). 1977